in search of
light and life

# VAGABOND
# TALES

a spiritual journey
## PLEASANT DESPAIN

# ALSO BY PLEASANT DESPAIN

in search of
light and life

# VAGABOND
# TALES

a spiritual journey
## PLEASANT DESPAIN

# COPYRIGHT AND CREDITS

Cover and Text Design:
Scott Jones, Chiang Mai, Thailand
Author photo: Chatri Chokthanyathon
Back cover photo: Richard Werner

For information or purchase of Vagabond Tales
and other books by Pleasant L. DeSpain,
please visit www.storypropress.com, www.amazon.com,
or August House, Inc. at www.augusthouse.com

## COVER PHOTO

A *Torii* is a traditional Japanese gateway marking the entrance
of a Shinto shrine symbolizing the transition from the secular
to the sacred. When walking through the gate, it is customary to bow
once and pass on the side, either right or left, but never the center.
It is believed that the shrine's deity resides at the center.

## DISCLAIMER

The practice of stillness, meditation and breathing techniques,
described herein, are based on my lifelong search for healing karma
and finding happiness. Please note that I'm not a psychologist,
guru, therapist, or medical professional. You are responsible
for how you choose to comprehend and use, or misuse, any of
my writings. I cannot accept responsibility for adverse effects
based on your physical, emotional, or spiritual health.

Listen to your higher self in all matters. If your self-examination
becomes uncomfortable, take care and proceed with caution.
Powerful emotions can be disruptive. If you have a history
of mental illness, please consult with your health care
professional before continuing.

# ACKNOWLEDGMENTS

My respect and appreciation to Scott Jones, my Chiang Mai, Thailand editor, whose professionalism, questions, insights, and suggestions brought this book up another three notches. When it comes to details and clarity in writing, Scott says, "I admit I'm a bit anal, as in anal-y-tical." It has been a pleasure working with Scott, my brother-by-choice.

Steve Floyd, CEO of August House, Inc., for believing in and supporting the story I've chosen to tell.

Lee Thomas, founder of Writers Without Borders in Chiang Mai. Several of these stories were read at Thursday night meetings and critiqued by attending authors.

# DEDICATION

*To my blessed family by birth, marriage, and choice,*
*and to my many teachers along the way.*
*This life and these stories wouldn't*
*have happened without you.*

*To all storytellers, amateur and professional.*
*We share a splendid passion and sacred path.*
*I believe in you.*

# CONTENTS

# Vagabond Tales

## INTRODUCTION

*I see it now. This world is swiftly passing.*
~The warrior Karna from the *Mahabharata*~

A VAGABOND MOVES FROM PLACE TO PLACE, going wherever impulse leads. The word's origin is from the Latin word vagary, to wander. A restless soul, I've wandered nearly my entire life, visited thirty-seven countries, lived in eight US states, and created home and hearth thirty-nine times. I've explored most of the United States and Canada, Mexico, Central America and Thailand. A true vagabond, I've usually traveled alone, with a mission to seek and find. My lasting treasures, discovered throughout my travels, are traditional and true stories of near and far.

Along the way, I helped create the modern profession of storyteller who makes a living sharing stories, old and new, made-up and true, aloud to listeners of most any age and enriching imaginations.

Along the way, I discovered meditation, going deeply within, and transcending our three-dimensional existence.

Along the way, I've met and befriended hundreds of like-minded souls. I've questioned the reasons people are born in these bodies, belong to a specific family, or grow up in Western or Eastern culture. I've always wanted to know how to best evolve as a human being, being human, and perhaps like you, I continue to seek answers to many eternal questions.

*What is the role of karma in my everyday life?*
*What is free in free will?*
*Do I live many lives, perpetually searching for answers?*
*Is happiness an illusion?*
*Must I find my soul mate to feel complete?*
*Is suffering a requirement of enlightenment?*
*What's the story here?*

I don't have the answers for everyone, nor should I. Your truths are as hard won as mine. My goal is to share my experiences. If you find a kindred spirit within these tales, let's smile together, realizing once again, we are never alone on our quest for light and life.

Thus, during the autumn of 1943, in the city of Denver, Colorado, I was born into this body. I inhaled deeply and let out a loud cry… the beginning of hardship, joy, and discovery.

[Some names and identifying details have been changed to protect the privacy of individuals.]

~ ~ ~

# Birth

## CHAPTER ONE

*A child is born
on the day and hour
when the celestial rays of light
are in mathematical
harmony with his
or her karma.*

~Sri Yukteswar~

# The Story

## Egypt

LONG AGO IN THE FABLED CITY OF ALEXANDRIA, a young king gathered his philosophers, architects, scientists, and artists in the grand and resplendent throne room. "Travel throughout the world," he proclaimed as he stretched out his arms. "Gather knowledge and bring it back to me. I wish to rule wisely."

Twenty years passed before the scholars returned with their discoveries and prepared their presentation in the royal palace. The number of books, artworks, specimens, and exhibits overwhelmed the middle-aged king.

"Ruling the kingdom takes much time and energy." He sighed and shook his head. "Condense this knowledge into a single volume. Then I'll read it and obtain the wisdom I seek."

Working day and night, his scholars required twenty more years to complete the project. Finally, they presented the aged king a heavy, leather-bound book containing hundreds of pages, inked on both sides.

The king received it with gladness, as well as sadness. "I'm old and tired and my legs no longer support me. My breath is short, and my eyes are weak. Bring me the storyteller."

Soon the teller of tales arrived and kneeled in front of the throne.

"Read this immense book, then come back and tell me the story," said the king. "I want the wisdom of the world before I die."

A week later, the storyteller returned to the palace and was led to the royal bedroom. Sitting on a simple wooden stool next to the bed, he told the frail king his tale. "My king, people are born, and they live. They learn and love along the way. They experience sorrow. They know joy. Some die young. Like you, many grow old before dying. Then once again, my king… they are born."

Moments after the tale was told and silence reigned in the room, the king passed away with a contented smile on his face.

~ ~ ~

# The Pool

## April 1983, San Diego, California

I BELIEVE WE ARRIVE ON THIS EARTH with a karmic story, a heavy weight on our hearts. For a fortunate few, it isn't a burden. For most of us, it's a necessary hardship.

On a blistering, Southern California afternoon, eight adults, women and men, were in the shallow end of a backyard swimming pool in the suburbs. I was nearly 40 years old and wearing a Speedo. We practiced "connected breathing," a difficult breath form requiring months of supervised experience in preparation for

Rebirthing. You learn to connect both the inhalation and exhalation in a circular breath.

Four of us hoped to relive our actual births in this life. We would have been naked but for the neighbor's sight lines. Rebirthing is better without clothing.

Stephanie was one of four breath coaches. I'd worked with her for a year, refining my connected breathing in an attempt to understand several mysteries of my current incarnation and resolve them. We both concluded I was ready for the final push—my birth experience.

Stephanie cradles my body in her strong arms, holding me so only my face remains above the sun-warmed water. I inhale a long, smooth breath to the count of seven heartbeats, and then exhale to seven more. At the bottom of each breath release, I begin the next inhale.

This breath form takes you out of your everyday existence. With clear intention, you can discover answers to complicated, personal questions. It's hard work, which requires focus, effort and a strong will. After ten to fifteen minutes, the breath takes over. Your breath breathes you rather than you doing the breathing. The release from the body, like an effortless detachment from three-dimensional reality, happens spontaneously, without drama. Breath carries consciousness to a larger dimension of your whole self, often dealing with the stated intention for the session. Your intentions need be clear, wise, solid, and true. It's a powerful and potentially dangerous practice, but with power comes risk, and with risk, there must be trust.

I trust Stephanie. She holds me close as I breathe consciously, over and over. Aware of being safe in her arms, suspended in the womb-warm water, I leave my physical being and travel to a place of complete surrender.

*I'm lying in a canoe tethered to shore with a long, ever-expanding rope. I'm safe in these waters, pushing forward. Every cell rejoices in the freedom of flowing beyond my body. I'm alive!*

Stephanie speaks softly. "All right, Pleasant?"

"Right." It is right.

*My intention floats into an awareness of my birth. Without pause, I'm in a different time and space. My body is gone. I'm in the State of Soul, completely aware. I'm not alone. Inundated by light, five guardians surround me—male and female, young and old, their bodies translucent. We're on a shelf of light high above Earth. Energy builds within. I'm returning to another life on Earth. Feelings of intense joy overwhelm me, but I'm confident.*

*"I'm ready. Let's go, let's go!" I hear myself say. I have no fear. Progress lay ahead.*

*My loving guides shower me with light. The lead guardian, male in form and feeling, whispers, "Your time is close. There will be difficulties. The road ahead is not easy. You're strong. Remember your goal. You will never be alone. We are with you, always."*

*The five embrace me with love. An electric current pulses throughout my being. My soul spirals down, down, toward our planet.*

*My physical body reacts in the pool as I wrap my arms tightly around my chest until I can hardly breathe. I feel a massive constriction along with a head-first, downward movement. I'm being born, fully aware of what's happening.*

*I'm thrilled, filled with energy and hope. The moment I'm pulled from my mother's body, my arms open wide in the pool. I re-experience my first inhalation, Inspiritus, taking spirit into my new existence.*

*The older male doctor hands me to a nurse and says, "He's small, but has all the right parts."*

*The nurse cleans my new body with a rough cloth, and then places me in my mother's arms. I grow cold but feel my mother's warm, welcome, unbounded love.*

*My father isn't at the hospital. I sense his disappointment in me since he was expecting a daughter. My brother had been born the year before. My father's disappointment will grow, culminating in a murderous rage many years later. That, however, is another story.*

*My awareness begins to fade. I cry out. "Aaaaiiee..."*

*"Good lungs," says the doctor.*

My new life, karma included, had begun.

~ ~ ~

## Time to Live

EVERY LIFE STORY has a beginning, middle, and end. Time exists on Earth to record not only the length of our lives, but also our life choices, actions, and experiences. It exists due to the nature of karma in everyday life. Karma is nature's response to action. Do good, get good in return. The opposite, too, is true, though karma doesn't judge good and evil in the Western concept of heaven and hell. Nor does karma forget—ever. Karma is what it is. My intensive study of the world's 12 major religions taught me that each one espouses the same first principle of living. "Do unto others as you would have them do unto you." Simple and true.

A universal archive exists in which the actions of all humans are recorded—the Akasha, the library of humanhood from the beginning of time. You have lived many lives. The most significant one is this one: your life, your story, the one where you presently exist in this three-dimensional reality. The one you helped create before your actual birth on Earth.

People choose to act, and then gain or lose according to their choices. It seems that our Creator likes stories. Imagine this—in the beginning, our Creator made a bold decision. By giving us the gift of choice, also called free will, with consequences directly tied to actions, the resulting stories would keep the cosmos entertained throughout time.

People like stories, too, and over the millennia, they've given God a plethora of names. Supreme Being, Lord, Allah, Brahma, YHWH (pronounced yah-weh), and Jehovah are just a few. I accept them all as valid and viable but prefer to use the word Creator from the Book of Isaiah: "God, the Creator of the world, is the One who created everything... the all-comprehending Being, the Maker and upholder of all things." I've heard it said that God created man is his own image, although I think a more accurate statement might be, "Man created God in his (or her) own image." When I use the word Creator, feel free to replace it with a word that resonates with you.

Time truly is relative, and no one's timeline is the same. Your current life may be brief or long, tragic or comic. It may be one of ironclad belief. "It's God's will. I'm not in control." Are you not in control of your destiny? Miraculously, you are. The Creator provided human life with the gift of manifestation. You create your reality based on your karmic history living this particular life.

Your goal is to evolve as a human being. It isn't easy, but possible. The pathway forward is to bring your karmic past into balance. Nature, here on Earth, requires balance. You are a natural being. You cannot escape that which you are. You cannot escape your karma, and karma never forgets. You have lived many lives and created many stories—tragedies or comedies or somewhere in between. Karma doesn't judge. You judge. People around you judge. If you were raised in the Western world, in one of the churches preaching their particular brand of right and wrong, you'd probably tend to be judgmental. It's in your DNA. You brought many of your judgments with you when you began this specific life-journey, and as you aged, a *pattern of judgment* emerged. Some folks might call this religion. I call it belief.

These words are what I believe, and help me share with you how I survive.

The acceptance or rejection of how you evolve, and the role that you play in the drama of all life, is the story of enlightenment. Acceptance of self is a key. Accepting and ultimately forgiving your judgments are major steps forward. You don't forgive with your mind, your words, or your broken heart. You can only forgive by coming into complete acceptance of your-whole-self.

You are "high-born." You wouldn't be reading this otherwise. High-born implies that you entered this life with earned gifts. You were loved. You were fed, clothed and sheltered. You learned. You socialized. You grew in age and experience. You've made it this far.

Not everyone is high-born in this lifetime. Many have suffered the challenges inherent in a lesser state of awareness and with fewer possibilities. In some lives, we choose a more difficult path to help balance our karma.

Being high-born, you and I were given a head start. Perhaps you asked important questions like I did…

*Who am I?*

*What is my role in this life?*

*Where am I headed?*

*Who loves me?*

*Whom will I choose to love?*

*What are my responsibilities in this life?*

*How do I make myself feel whole?*

*Why do I not get on with my father, mother, brother, sister, child?*

*Why am I unhappy, depressed, and unfulfilled?*

*What is the role of my family, both blood and chosen, in this life?*

*Why did this disease choose me?*

*Did I choose it?*

*Am I to blame?*

*Why did I bring on this suffering?*

*Why is life so damn hard?*

*Does God exist?*

*Is there an afterlife?*

*How do I survive my addictions?*

*Have I failed?*

*Have I succeeded even partially?*

Every question is relevant, but the answer to all of them is not, "It's God's will." Nor is it, "I don't know." If you are high-born you have the answers but often ask the wrong questions. The question is not why, but how. How do you forgive your past actions in this life and former lives and accept your-whole-self this time around? That's what you have come to accomplish. This particular journey begins and ends and will inevitably begin again. Start with the heart.

Herein lies the State of Soul. Your soul enters your body with your initial breath. The Greeks called it *In-spiritus*—the taking in of spirit. Your soul departs your body with your final breath—*Expiritus*. Your first inhalation as a baby not only brings in the breath of life, but also the state of your individual soul and the DNA of the heart. Your heart carries the weight of your past, the potential of your future lives, your light *and* your dark.

No story exists without a cast of characters. We're all in this life-production together. Lungs pumping spirit into the body, each actor bursts into the latest role in the next act of their karmic journey, live on Stage Earth. Every life has a major backstory, that mystery each of us is born to solve and resolve. Three-dimensional selves ordinarily do not have access to such vital information upon birth. If you choose to take evolutionary steps forward, you must start to understand and accept the state of your soul—warts and all.

I've been on this journey for many years, and still have, in the words of Robert Frost, "miles to go before I sleep." I'm not *enlightened*, but I do experience more light in my everyday life than before. I'm old, healthy, and happy. I'm blessed with family and friends throughout the wide world. I've traveled inward as well as outward, manifesting failures and successes. I've fully accepted my-whole-self, my past lives, as well as the past and present of my current life. Today, I do love being the human being I've become.

That love has made me smile as I've been writing these words... And now, feeling the joy that comes with acceptance, I'm laughing aloud, from and with the heart reverberating throughout the universe. No one hears me. I'm alone, but not alone. Oh, the stories I wish to share with you, dear reader. Let's do the work of healing our karma together.

~ ~ ~

# Family

## CHAPTER TWO

*If you
cannot get rid
of the family skeleton,
you may as well
make it dance.*

~George Bernard Shaw~

# Pulling the Rope

## America

IN 1770, SAMUEL FORBES BUILT A HOUSE AND BARN near Canaan located in the northwest corner of Connecticut. Soon afterward he fell in love with Lucy, the daughter of a local farmer named Amos Pierce. Samuel asked him for permission to court his daughter, but Amos didn't feel that Samuel was the right man for his Lucy, and said no.

Lucy wasn't a typical girl of that time. She didn't enjoy baking or household chores. She'd never been handy with a needle and thread. And she hated to wear frilly dresses. She was a strong woman and made way her in the world as well as any man. When she wrestled with her brothers, she left them lying in the mud. She pitched hay and built fences, raced horses and hunted game.

She never said, "I think so." She'd say, "Yes, that's what I'll do. Trust me. I'll get it done.

She never said, "Yes, Mother, whatever you decide." She'd say, "That's my decision, and I'm sticking to it."

She was a force unto herself.

Smitten with Samuel, Lucy felt he'd make a good husband. Her father's decision disappointed her, but only hardened her resolve. She approached him as he split wood behind the shed. "Father, I need to speak with you."

"What is it?" he asked, wiping the sweat off his forehead and furrowing his brow.

"Samuel Forbes is a good man. I love him and want him to court me."

Father Amos grew rigid. "Daughter, I already said no." He buried the axe head in an oak log to emphasize his decision.

"Well…" A thin grin crept across Lucy's face as she paused. She'd seen this coming. "I've decided to marry him, no matter what you say."

He crossed his sinewy arms over his chest and glared down at her. "Not while you live under my roof you won't!"

"Thank you for making it plain, Father." She turned away and marched toward the stable.

"Then you'll obey me," her father demanded, brandishing the axe above his head, "and stop this nonsense about Samuel?"

"No." Lucy threw her words backwards over her shoulder. "I'm moving out from under your roof!"

She saddled her stallion and galloped across the verdant valley to Samuel's farm and into her lover's arms. After discussing the situation, they vowed to elope that very afternoon. Gleeful and huddled together on the wooden bench of Samuel's buggy, they traveled down to the state of New York and found a justice of the peace to do the honors.

On their way home, with Canaan in sight on the horizon, the newlyweds chatted merrily while envisioning their life together.

As the discussion of their roles got more specific, treading on sensitive ground, Lucy pinpointed a stark disagreement. In her inimitable style, she spoke like a stone. "I hope you realize that no man will ever tell me what to do."

"My dear, be reasonable," Samuel pleaded as he cracked the whip over the horse's head, "You know that every husband sets the rules of the household."

Lucy scoffed at the notion and slid to the far side of the seat. "You can set all the rules you want. Just don't expect me to follow them."

"Then how will we get along together?" he asked, shaking his head.

"It will be best if I make the rules and you follow them." She crossed her arms across her chest, just like her father.

"Is that fair?"

"Husband, I am as strong as you, and I can run the farm as well as you. Why shouldn't I rule the roost?"

Samuel got quiet for a while and then sighed, "Okay, sweetheart. Let's have a contest of strength when we get home. If you win, you'll be in charge. If I win, I'll make the rules."

Lucy smirked and heartily accepted the challenge. "Agreed."

Immediately upon arriving home, Samuel tossed a long rope up and over the roof of the barn.

"You pull from one side, and I'll pull from the other," he explained. "Whoever pulls the entire rope over the barn is the strongest—the winner! Do you still agree, my love?"

"Yes, Samuel, I agree. Let the contest begin!"

They took their places on each side of the barn. Samuel shouted the signal, "On your mark. Get set. Go!" And the tug o' war began.

Lucy pulled with all her might and failed to yank the rope over to her side. Samuel pulled with all his strength but couldn't budge the rope. Neither could best the other, and the rope still straddled the barn's roof.

"Lucy!" hollered Samuel. "Come round to my side of the barn! I have a new plan that I think you'll like."

Her curiosity tweaked, she dropped her end of the rope and ambled around to her husband.

Samuel offered his end to Lucy. "Grab hold of the rope with me. Let's pull together."

With four arms pumping in unison, they yanked the rope over the barn in a few seconds. It fell in a coil on the ground in front of them.

Samuel placed a victorious foot on the pile as if they'd just conquered a timber rattlesnake. "Let that be the way we run our house! We'll pull together from now on."

Lucy beamed, wrapped his arm around her waist, and pecked him on the cheek. "You are very wise, husband of mine."

Working together, they sweated, laughed, and prospered on their land.

Years later, the day after the birth of their second child, Lucy and Samuel received a surprise visit from her father.

"I was wrong about Samuel," Amos admitted. "He's a good man. I can see now what you felt in your heart so long ago. Please forgive my stubbornness, daughter. I want us to be a family again."

Lucy hugged her father and whispered in his ear. "I've missed you."

As one big happy family, they all shared long and fulfilling lives.

~ ~ ~

# Family Values

*In my mid-twenties, I changed my first name Jerry to Pleasant, which honored my ancestors and made me the fifth generation "Pleasant" in the DeSpain family.*

## Denver, Colorado, 1941–1956

AT THE AGE OF EIGHTEEN MONTHS, I lived in a modest house on Chase Street in a friendly, working-class neighborhood filled with large families and lots of kids. Dad was away in the US Air Force as World War II wound down in 1945. My two-and-a-half-year-old brother and I were home alone with Mom.

On a sunny spring morning, Mom went into the backyard, emptied the smoldering, white-hot ashes from the coal stove into the dirt, and returned to the kitchen. While brother Bobby played with the dog in the front yard, I toddled around back and plopped down into the glowing ashes. Shock paralyzed my small body and my vocal cords. I couldn't stand up or even scream. I just sat and burned.

Somehow feeling that something was wrong, Mom ran out the front door and yelled to Bobby, "Where's your brother?"

Bobby pointed to the backyard. She raced around the house to find me slumped over, head to chest, motionless. My left shoe and sock had vanished. My blue corduroy overalls were scorched and charred up to my tiny waist. In a panic, Mom yanked me from the ashes and carried me to the house next door. Our neighbor agreed to watch Bobby. Mom threw me over her shoulder and ran a half mile until she could wave down a stranger's car and get me to the hospital.

In the emergency room, the doctor explained the grim diagnosis to my mother. "Your son has suffered third-degree burns over thirty percent of his body. And right now . . . he's in deep shock."

Mom choked out her questions. "Can't you help him? Will he recover?"

"I think he'll live," the doctor said, "but he won't walk."

Miracles do happen. Dad pleaded with his military superiors for help, and I was admitted to Colorado's, Fitzsimmons Army Hospital in Aurora, Colorado. A skilled surgeon removed layers of skin from my back and thighs, and grafted them, piece by piece, onto my burnt legs. Everyone hoped. Everyone prayed.

I learned to walk again, not once, but three times. Skin grafts do not grow with the body, and I underwent three more re-grafting operations during the next ten years. My balance was a bit off, but I was upright and mobile.

My parents, Robert and
Eleanor DeSpain, both
beautiful and in love, married in Golden, Colorado
in 1941. Handsome, phys-
ically strong, and nine-
teen years old, Robert was
a high school wrestling
champion. Eleanor, strik-
ingly attractive with high
cheekbones and cascad-
ing black hair, left school
before graduating to be
married at age seventeen.

Mom and Dad

One year later my older brother arrived and was named
Bobby after my dad. After I entered the world in 1943,
we moved to the house on Chase Street. Brother Roger
joined the family two years later in 1945.

Dad made a living as a carpenter, while Mom stayed
home raising three rambunctious boys. Dad's mother
moved in with us and lived in a converted chicken
coop in the backyard. Grandma had a kitchen, bedroom, and bathroom, and enjoyed her privacy. Bobby
called her Mamaw, which rhymes with Grandma, and
the name stuck. After that, everyone referred to her
as Mamaw. She helped around the house, make tasty
biscuits for breakfast, and taught Mom how to sew,
cook, clean, and do all those things that grandmothers
do best.

When I was about seven, the six of us gathered in
the backyard to drink sun-tea and play ball on a Sunday afternoon. Mom and Mamaw sipped their cold
tea on the sidelines under a shade tree and shared the

neighborhood gossip. Dad stood at bat and peppered hard drives to us kids spread across the grass.

Tossing the baseball up into the air, Dad hollered, "Heads up, Bobby."

Crack! The ball flew into Bobby's right-hand mitt, halfway across the yard.

"Good catch, son." Dad congratulated him with a cock of his head. "Heads up, Jerry! This one's for you."

Crack! The next ball whizzed past my outstretched glove, flew over the fence, and bounced down the alley. Chasing after it, I heard Dad yell, "Dammit, Jerry, you gotta try harder!"

Dad gently bunted the next ball young Roger, who grabbed it up from the ground with ease.

"Good goin', kid. We'll make a shortstop out of you, yet."

There wasn't much in the way of art, music, and books in our house. The main decoration was a full-size bearskin, head intact, hanging on the wall above the living room sofa. Dad was a hunter and this rug was his pride and joy. He wanted his progeny to become athletes, fishermen, and hunters like him, what he called 'real men.'

"Boys don't cry," he often repeated.

I did cry at night. My legs hurt. Growing pains during the healing process. Skin grafts don't grow as readily as natural skin. They can stretch, break, or bleed. My grafts might have been numb, but plenty of lively nerves surrounded them.

Mom kept a tidy house, sewed most of our clothes, prepared nourishing meals, and read us Bible stories at bedtime. We three boys had learned our letters and numbers before entering preschool. Dad came home from work, tired and dirty, Monday through Friday, and cleaned up before dinner. As we sat together at the table, I knew four things. Mom and Dad loved each other. My brothers and I were loved. Our big black Labrador, Butch, was loved. And Mamaw made our family complete.

Left to right: Roger, Bobby, Jerry

The 1940s were the golden age of radio. For our household entertainment, we gathered to listen and laugh at Jack Benny, Red Skelton, Burns and Allen, and Amos and Andy. My brothers and I relished the adventures of *Jack Armstrong, the All-American Boy, Tom Mix,* and *The Cisco Kid.* After listening to each adventure, I loved to imagine myself far beyond our world on Chase Street.

One Saturday morning Mom and Dad bundled Roger into our Ford station wagon to take him to the doctor. "We won't be gone long, boys," Dad said. "Behave yourselves." They left Bobby, age 9, in charge.

Once the parents were out the door, I proposed a

fun scenario. "Let's put on our swimsuits and play Tarzan!"

We pushed out the chairs from the dining room table. Lying on small kitchen rugs as our rafts, we negotiated the wilds of a jungle river with rubber, play knives clenched in our teeth.

I directed the unfolding events. "Look out for the python on the tree to your right, Bobby!"

My brother made me proud, pretending to wrestle with the giant snake and slicing off its head with his knife.

"Oh, no! The natives are throwing spears," I yelled. "We have to get out of here!"

How quickly we maneuvered throughout the dining room on our rafts!

"There's a gorilla behind the trees," I whispered. "Let's hide under the waterfall."

We paddled back under the table and waited for the beast to leave. But he didn't leave. The plot thickened. The gorilla was right next to me.

Bobby declared, "I'm the gorilla, Jerry, and I'm going to kill you!"

"No, no, no!" I started to play-fight with him. We got into it and official wrestling commenced. I escaped his hold, stood up, and grabbed Bobby by an arm and leg. I tried to swing him around but couldn't handle his weight. I let go and he smashed into a chair, head first. Bobby and the chair toppled to the ground.

Fate stepped in through the front door, in the form of the rest of family.

"What the hell!" Dad's red face looked like it might explode.

Blood poured from a cut above Bobby's right eye. Using a kitchen dishcloth to staunch the flow, Mom said, "Put Bobby in the car, Bob. This is bad."

Before leaving for his second trip to the doctor, Dad growled through pursed lips that matched his pursed eyes, "You're in trouble, Jerry. Get dressed, clean up the mess, and straighten up the dining room."

Bobby got several stitches above his right eye and carries the scar to this day. I got spanked, especially hard, but the only scars are in my heart.

My brothers and I played with neighborhood kids and occasionally got into trouble. We'd ride our bikes ten blocks down to "The Creek," run through the fields, and get lost in the woods. One Saturday Torpie and his younger brother, David, showed us how to catch garter snakes.

"Can we keep 'em?" asked Bobby.

"Sure," Torpie said. "Put 'em in water, and they'll be fine."

With five garter snakes in a coffee can, we rode home to find Dad gone and Mom chatting with Mamaw in the backyard. We discussed what to do with our treasure haul from the creek.

"Should we fill the tub?" I asked.

"No, the sink," said Bobby.

Roger chimed in with glee. "I get to open the can."

That's when the panic began, not only for the reptiles, but also for my brothers and me. After splashing into the sink, the snakes stiffened and leaped out onto the floor in five different directions. Zoom, they were gone!

We searched the entire house. No snakes.

"Are we in trouble?" Roger asked.

"I think we should tell Mom," I said.

Bobby agreed with Roger but disagreed with me. "No. Don't say anything. The snakes will find a way out of the house."

Two days later, we heard Mom's shriek when one slithered out the vacuum hose in the hall closet. She found two more under Roger's bed and demanded an explanation.

We told the truth. Mom and her Posse of Three crept around together until we found the remaining unwelcome guests: one behind the sofa and the other under the kitchen sink. Luckily, snakes are slower on land than in the water. We swept them up and set them free in the alley.

Dad the Disciplinarian heard about our adventure that evening. "Bobby, get my belt."

I always heard these words before a spanking, but never believed them. Sure enough, they came again, and I didn't believe them.

"This is going to hurt me more than you, son."

In 1952, we were the last family on our block to afford a television. With a minuscule, black and white screen, encased in an enormous wooden console, it arrived on a Saturday afternoon. That was a momentous day.

I'd watched Jackie Gleason's hour-long show at friends' houses, but on this special night, it would play in our living room. We three boys sat on the sofa with the bear-skin rug above our heads, guzzling Cokes between mouthfuls of salty homemade popcorn. Mom and Dad, in their respective chairs on either side of the couch, sipped wine. The glowing console resided in splendor at the far end of the room, and at last, *The Cavalcade of Stars* began.

With five pairs of eyes glued to the screen, we laughed at "The Honeymooners" sketch starring Alice and Ralph Kramden. After an endless commercial for Nescafe Instant Coffee, the big band played, the curtains opened, and the June Taylor Dancers appeared.

A dozen gorgeous young women wearing short skirts kicked their long legs high!

A curious thing happened as the dancing progressed. Wanting a better view, Dad slowly scooted his chair closer and closer to the television screen. He made it halfway across the living room.

"Bob!" Mom hollered. "What do you think you're doing?"

That was one of the few times in my young life when I saw Dad's face turn red from embarrassment rather than anger.

A few years later, a family with four hard-bitten boys moved into our neighborhood. It wasn't long before they challenged my brother—now called Bob like our dad—and me to a fistfight. Bob kept a level head and refused to fight. I was scared.

Dad felt the tension in the house and asked us, "Okay, what's going on?" After we shared the details, he took us into his bedroom, out of younger Roger's hearing. "Do you know what the family jewels are?"

"No," I said.

"You mean our balls?" asked Bob.

"Right. The most vulnerable part of a guy is his testicles… his nuts. So, kick this kid as hard as you can in the balls, and he'll drop to the ground. Then run like hell! He'll never bother you again."

This man-to-man conversation was our entire self-defense education, as well as the only "birds and bees" talk.

I'd felt safe in our little house from the time I was born. I knew love and discipline, homework and chores. I knew my place as the middle child, the often-cautioned dreamer. I'd never be as athletic as my brothers, but I believed I'd be all right if I kept my head down and did my best.

Dad, the provider, and Mom, the caretaker, were solid in their respective family roles until a shift occurred. A series of deep earthquakes. The foundation of our lives began to crumble.

"It's midnight, Bob!" Mom yelled. "Why were you out so late?"

"Calm down, Eleanor. You'll wake the kids."

I was awake in my bedroom, hearing all, and not for the first time.

"The union meeting finished an hour ago, and I stopped to have a beer with friends."

"Liar! Who were you with? What's her name?"

"Don't call me a liar. Shut up and go back to bed."

Brother Bob began spending more time out of the house, playing sports at school and with his friends. I disappeared into science fiction and adventure novels checked out from the Denver Public Library. Roger stopped speaking, sometimes for days at a time.

One Saturday morning, the family, including Ma-maw, sat around the table eating breakfast. Mom dished out the last of the French toast.

"Bob, I'm short of cash. The milkman needs to be paid, and I have to shop for groceries."

"I gave you enough money last Friday," Dad grunted.

"No, you didn't. You were short by ten dollars."

"I can give you five bucks. It's all I have."

He reached for his wallet, but Mom was on him. "What about the fifty you've hidden under the visor in the station wagon?"

Dumbstruck, we all stared at Dad. Fifty dollars in the 1950s was worth five hundred in today's marketplace.

Dad scowled in silence. His guilt was palpable.

"I searched the car at three this morning, Bob. Were you saving it for one of your new friends?"

"Oh, that money," he managed to say. "I'd forgotten about it."

"Of course, you had, dear." She put an extra emphasis on the word "dear."

Without missing a beat, Mom turned to us boys. "Help me wash the dishes, and then we'll go shopping. First on the list are new tennis shoes for all of you."

Dad left the table in defeat. He stomped to his bedroom and slammed the door shut.

Mamaw whispered, loud enough for all to hear, "Good for you, Eleanor."

The next incriminating incident occurred two months later. Dad arrived home on a Sunday afternoon wearing a suave brown leather jacket. Western in style with fringes on the sleeves and back, it fit him perfectly.

"Where'd you get that?" demanded Mom.

"Don't you worry about it."

"How much did it cost?"

"Not one nickel. It didn't fit my carpenter friend, and he gave it to me." Dad left the room and busied himself in the bedroom.

Mom looked at me and asked, "Whoever heard of a lady carpenter?"

She waited until the following Friday afternoon to exact her revenge. When I got home from school, she said, "Honey, do me a favor. Get your Dad's new leather jacket from our closet."

"Why?"

"He'll want to wear it to the carpenters meeting tonight, and I've decided to make some alterations."

She laid the jacket on the dining room table next to her formidable silver pinking shears. I watched in amazement as she went to work. The fringes were the first to go, followed by removal of the sleeves. The soft leather collar went next, and finally, she cut the body of the coat into four wide strips.

My eyes were probably as wide as they'd ever been. "Dad's gonna be mad."

"I think so, too. Take this mess out to the barrel. I'll get the paper and matches."

The remains of his gift were burned beyond recognition. Dad got home from work on time, ate dinner with us, and freshened up in the bathroom. Dressed in slacks and a nice shirt, he waltzed out of the bedroom and asked, "Eleanor, where's my new jacket?"

"You might want to look in the barrel out back."

Not one kind word passed between them during the miserable year that followed. Often absent from our home and our lives, Dad left a sadness in his wake. Divorce, rare in the 1950s, marked a failed family.

In 1956, I went to my annual appointment with the surgeon who'd saved my life and legs eleven years earlier. After the examination, Dr. Blanford said, "You're still growing, and may need one more operation."

That process would mean three weeks in the hospital, hundreds of stitches sewing the patchwork of fresh skin shaved from my body, and weeks of convalescence with both legs encased hip to ankle in metal braces. I'd suffer through protracted pain and have another battle with gravity.

I gave him a firm answer. "I don't want it."

"I understand how you feel, but like the last time, if the skin breaks and you bleed, you'll have no choice."

"Can I make it stretch?"

"Possibly. Run a bit every day, but don't overdo it. See me in six months, and we'll know if it's working."

My best friend in the neighborhood since kindergarten, Duane came to the rescue. We'd shared bikes, fishing poles, newspaper delivery routes, and jokes throughout our young lives.

"Sloan's Lake," said Duane. "Two and a half miles around. We'll run it every morning."

"What time?"

"Six-thirty. Then home for breakfast. We'll make it to school on time."

He showed up at my door in the early morning. We raced our bikes the dozen city blocks to the lake, dropped them in the grass, and stretched our legs.

"Ready to run?" Duane asked.

"No, but let's go."

For the next three months, we ran. We kept a moderate pace around the lake without stopping. Stretching skin hurts. When I complained, my mentor, buddy, and daily doctor reminded me of my mission. We kept going. My muscles grew, and the grafted skin didn't break. I didn't need that final surgery.

On my first day in junior high school, the physical education coach blew his whistle to get our attention. "Line up boys and listen good. You're going to shower after gym class every day. No exceptions. When I send you to the locker room, get naked, look at each other's peckers, and get over it."

I'd been naked with boys my age in other locker rooms. I wasn't ashamed of my thin body, nor was I proud. New guys had called me out before.

"Man, what happened? You run through fire? That's ugly."

"Didn't your mother tell you not to play with matches?"

"You know you walk a little funny, right?"

Fortunately, it was a small junior high school, and once a comment was made, there was no need to repeat it. My athletic brother Bob, an eighth grader, made certain no one bullied me.

At the end of class, the coach blew his whistle again. "Hit the showers, boys!"

I was familiar with the smells of sweat, rot, and disinfectant permeating the plastered walls and moldy wooden benches of the old school's locker room. Everyone stripped off their gym clothes and pushed to be first into the rectangular, concrete room. A dozen shower heads stuck out from the walls. Only ten worked.

As I soaped up, one of the new guys hung his towel on a peg, entered the wet room, and chose the shower head next to mine. Shaggy blond hair, startling blue eyes, and better built than most seventh graders, he was a boy to envy.

"Who are you?" he asked.

"Jerry. You?"

"Nate. Use your soap?"

"Sure."

"Your legs? What happened?"

"I was burned."

"Your balls? They okay?"

"They're as big as yours."

Shouting over the noise of the showers, Nate yelled, "Hey guys, Jerry's balls are as big as mine!"

Everyone laughed, including me.

"Thanks for the soap, man."

Grinning, I thought, I like him.


Brother Bob played football, basketball, baseball, and learned to wrestle. The little kid who was told he'd never walk joined the track team. After practice one afternoon, the locker room filled with guys from all three middle-school grades. The track coach was dealing with one runner's sprained ankle.

"Listen up, boys!" he bellowed. "I'm taking David to the nurse's office. Shower, get dressed, and go home. Charlie, you're in charge."

"Okay, Coach."

As soon as he was naked, Charlie joined several of us who were already showering. I didn't understand why he had towels draped over his arm until he and a friend used them to block the floor drains. A six-inch lip crossed the wide entrance to the shower room, and the water level quickly rose.

Whooping and howling, Charlie and his friend lay down, slid across the floor, and bounced off the walls. Within a minute, our improvised shower pool sported teenage boys flying through the shallow water, rubbing against each other, and slapping the walls. Nate wrapped his arms around me from behind. Locked together, we sped the length of the room. It felt great until I hit the wall with my head.

"Ouch."

Releasing me from his grip, Nate asked, "You okay?"

"Yeah. This is fun!"

Pointing at each other's semi-erections, aware we weren't the only ones enjoying the eroticism, we joined the chorus of laughter.

Suddenly the coach returned. "What the hell? Turn off the water and pull the plugs! Everyone out of the showers! Now! Charlie, you're in big trouble!"

Hands covering groins, we obeyed.

I was puzzled. Like other guys, I noticed girls and thought I liked them. I wasn't queer. I didn't even know exactly what queer meant except that it was beyond bad, truly deplorable, an eternity in hell. My feelings for Nate bothered me. I didn't want sex with another guy, but if Nate wanted to mess around?

Home from school on a Friday afternoon, I wasn't surprised to find Mom on the sofa squeezing a handful of tissues. Bob and Roger were beside her. Dad had moved out the month before, and legalities of the divorce were being handled in court.

Mom dried her eyes, sighed, and reached out to me. "Sit with us, Jerry. We have to talk."

I sat.

"Your Dad and I met with a judge today. Each of you will have to decide who you want to live with."

"Where's he going to live?" I asked.

"An apartment somewhere."

"I'm staying with you, Mom."

Bob and Roger said in unison, "Me, too."

"Good. Your Dad's agreed to provide us with some money each month. We'll make it, but it's going to be hard. I'll learn to drive and get a job. You three will have to help me with the shopping and keeping the house clean." She shook her finger at us while still holding a soggy tissue. "And you can't get into trouble. Otherwise, the judge can take you away from me. Promise me!"

We all promised.

"Does Dad want us to go with him?" Bob asked timidly.

"No... not really."

"That's what I thought," he said as his head drooped onto his chest.

They finalized the divorce two months later. Dad married his Catholic girlfriend the following week. To avoid church doctrine regarding second marriages, he told the priest that he was childless.

When I heard those words at age thirteen, I swore never to fear, respect, or love my father again. That vow lasted for twenty-seven years.

~ ~ ~

# Pulling Together

*A bond between souls is ancient*
*—older than the planet.*
~Dianna Hardy~

SAMUEL AND LUCY FORBES PULLED TOGETHER, but Bob and Eleanor DeSpain spent years unraveling the rope. Some families succeed, others fail. It's not by accident that parents meet, fall in love, raise children, and live happily—or unhappily—ever after. I've learned that reasons for success or failure exist beyond our three-dimensional world.

I was fortunate to meet Ida Rose Barber, a wise woman-of-age. She lived alone in her substantial house on Seattle's Capitol Hill and loved entertaining young people searching for answers to life's perplexing questions. She'd studied at the University of Chicago in the 1940s with Count Alfred Korzybski, the renowned Polish-American scholar who developed and named the field of General Semantics. His book—*Science and Sanity: An Introduction to General Semantics*—was on my graduate studies reading list and explored the study of human communication and the difficulties we have with speech and language. Ida Rose Barber's book—

*The Pink Elephant, Something About General Semantics*—was published by Vantage Press of New York in 1968.

During the summer of 1973, I'd been invited to an intimate social gathering at Ida Rose's elegant home. Wearing a muted green, tailored gown with a shimmering silk scarf draped around her shoulders, Ida Rose welcomed me at the door. She was poised yet relaxed and cheerful. Framed with whimsical curls of white and grey hair, her face exuded kindness.

"You must be the storyteller. And what a wonderful name you have, Pleasant DeSpain. Come in, come in. Let me introduce you to the others."

She led me into her tastefully furnished living room, highlighted with artwork, antiques, bookshelves packed with serious titles and heavy tomes, 18th and 19th century Persian rugs to cushion every step, and a black Steinway grand piano. The décor was as impressive as my host. I shook hands and traded names with the other eight guests.

I sat on a massive Victorian sofa, set my wine glass on a coaster resting atop an exquisitely carved wooden box, and raved to the man next to me, "This is so beautiful!"

"It was Teddy Roosevelt's campaign chest," he explained, and the sofa you're sitting on belonged to Calvin Coolidge. He then pointed to the other side of the room. "And those two black lacquer cabinets were Napoleon Bonaparte's!"

"Amazing," I sighed. The whole environment felt exotic and wealthy, filled with light and a sense of calm. I felt safe and warm.

At one point, Ida Rose's hazel eyes sparkled with passion as she shared a bit of her past with the group. "I traveled to Chicago to study with the Count because

I wanted to find some way to explain me to myself!"

I knew I was in the right place. And I wanted to return. At the party's end, I approached Ida Rose. "I wonder if it would be possible to meet with you privately?"

"Oh, yes, Pleasant. I'm very interested in your work. Would tea at three on Tuesday fit into your schedule?"

"That would be wonderful. It's been a pleasure to meet you, and an education! I'll see you again next week."

While driving to Ida Rose's magnificent home the following Tuesday, I pondered what we might discuss. My storytelling involved communication using a variety of methods including imagination, breath, words, emotions, and pacing. And it seemed to fit into the category of General Semantics. I hoped to gain insight from the master. I didn't realize was how much of, nor how broad an education I was about to receive.

She greeted me at the door, escorted me into the living room, and gestured to the sofa. Once again, Calvin's sofa was over-stuffed and rather uncomfortable, but kept me upright, polite, and orderly in true Victorian style. It was not made for a nap.

Ida Rose handed me a white linen napkin and then poured tea from a white Chinese pot into delicate porcelain cups decorated with blue butterflies. I set my cup on Teddy's chest. She placed her teapot and cup on a small circular table next to her stately light-blue winged chair with thin white stripes and sat facing me.

"Now, what's on your mind, Pleasant? What would you like to talk about today?"

"Communication. I want to better understand my audiences, and what they need from me."

"Maybe you don't see the obvious, dear."

"What am I missing?"

"Human beings fail at communication. We discriminate against each other and continue to fight wars. It's always been so and will carry on unless we change our thinking and speaking."

"Change it how?"

"Take responsibility for what we say and do. We have the gift of 'free will.' But that gift is also a curse. We've abused it from the beginning of time, and the way things are going, it appears we'll continue to do so." Ida Rose gazed into the middle distance for a moment, and then continued. "It's a big story, Pleasant, one that few people have heard, let alone understand. An old Spanish proverb says it all, 'Take what you want but pay for it.' We act on our free will, and those actions create consequences."

"Karma?" I asked.

"They call it karma in the East. I call it 'paying your dues.' Here's an important fact about actions and consequences." She paused for effect. "*The universe doesn't forget.* After you die in this life, the universe remembers who you were, what you did, and what must be fully justified."

"But how can you pay them back if you're dead?"

"Our bodies perish, not our souls, nor the memories of our actions."

"So, I guess we come back in another life to pay our dues?"

"Basically, yes."

"How do I know what is owed? I don't remember a former life. I don't know what I did or didn't do."

"Exactly, but the universe remembers."

"I'm confused."

Ida Rose's sweet laugh surprised me. "Of course, dear boy. Who wouldn't be confused hearing this for the first time? The universe never forgets and demands retribution along the way to keep the scales of justice in balance."

"But what if we run out of time?"

"Hmm. Run out of time? That's a relative question. Time, as we experience it, was created for the earth. Einstein's general theory of relativity established time as a physical thing, part of space-time—the gravitational field produced by massive objects. But perhaps time is nothing except a measure of change, something that exists only as long as there are changes… or debts to pay. If you don't pay off your credit card at the end of the month, you continue paying the next month. What do you think happens when you die?"

"Are you saying that I might live many lives to pay back my past actions?"

"Oh, yes. As many as it takes."

"Let's look at a bigger picture. Do you believe in God or a higher power?"

"Yes."

"Are you referring the God you learned about in church, or of consciousness itself?"

"I'd say… consciousness itself."

"Good. Consciousness is everything we see and don't see. The universe is consciousness. An intelligence beyond human understanding—which I call the Deity—created Earth millions of years ago with the Big Bang. And the Deity must have thought, 'What would happen if I gave human beings choice, free will, and the ability to manifest?' Now that would be an interesting experiment."

"I think we've misused free will."

"Yes, terribly so. If you handed the keys to a bright red sports car to a 14-year-old boy who had never driven before, and told him to have fun, just imagine the carnage! We've been given unlimited power to do good or evil. But the Deity decided that power comes with responsibility, and unfortunately, humans haven't been able to develop the critical judgment to handle power."

"So, take what you want but pay for it."

"Just so. And the universe, dear boy, requires payment in full. That's how karma works."

"Let me see if I have this straight. I came into this life full of memories I don't remember, and I have to make amends? And it might take many lives to pay back for my past actions?"

"Challenging, isn't it? Our souls agreed to participate in the Earth experiment." Ida Rose finished her tea and toasted with her raised teacup. "And we must finish what we started, but that's enough for today, dear. Come back in two weeks, and we'll talk further."

We shared tea for two several times over the course of a year. In one significant encounter, our discussion led to my family history and emerging career. She'd absorbed quite a bit about me during our chats and had been kind enough to attend two of my storytelling events in Seattle. We always settled into the same living room scene. Tea, sofa, winged chair, and the solid, silent Steinway like a sentinel stationed in her inner sanctum.

"Why do people fall in love, get married, and have children," I asked, "only to end in divorce and bitterness?"

"We all have mental pictures or ideas of life on Earth. It's what we in General Semantics call *the map*. We call the reality of life *the territory*. And Count Korzybski's most famous dictum is 'The map is not the territory.'

"Your folks probably had ritualistic ideas of marriage, the dream of loving each other forever and working together to create a wonderful life. I'm sure your mom had her dream, and your dad had his, similar but not the same. And neither of their maps could stand up to the hard reality of adult life. *The territory always rules*. Your parents were right to separate and get on with their lives. It's when we stick to our old, outdated maps that we run into trouble."

"Why do we make maps?"

"It's in our nature. Humans are mapmakers who gather information from our five senses. We build preferences, which I call prejudices, on what we experience and then project them onto the world about us. We want the world to function exactly as we've planned it, but it doesn't. The only way to find happiness is to change our maps. You've told me about your parents, and your childhood. How are your mother and father doing now?"

"Well, Dad's still married to his second wife, and it's been seventeen years. They support each other and seem happy. Mom married a wonderful man fifteen years ago, and I've gained three more siblings. I know Mom and Gene, my stepdad, love each other."

"What does your dad say about your mom?"

"I've never heard him bad mouth her."

"And Mom about Dad?"

"She despises him, still."

"It seems your dad changed his map and got on with his life. Your mom was fortunate to find a man whose map aligns with hers and has the potential to move forward, but unless she forgives your dad, she'll be unhappy. How's her health?"

"Good overall, except for migraine headaches that keep her in bed for days."

"That may be the result of having her first 'marriage map' destroyed. Bitterness is a heavy burden. Let's talk about your maps, Pleasant. How do you get on with your birth father?"

"I don't despise him, but I don't like him, either. We have independent lives. He doesn't ask about mine, and I don't care about his."

"It sounds like your *child-parent map* still lives. Created during the time of innocence, many 'shoulds' embedded themselves in your DNA. Fathers 'should' work hard and support the family. Mothers 'should' stay at home and raise the kids. Children 'should' experience the same world as their parents. It's how our prejudices are created. Religions, governments, and even neighborhoods fight to hold on to their maps. They don't like someone insisting, 'My map's better than yours. My map's truer than yours. You should use my map instead of yours.' But the map isn't the territory, and all these 'shoulds' result in discrimination and wars."

I raised both hands, palms up, fingers stretched out in search of the answer. "When will we ever learn?"

Ida Rose chuckled. "When we decide to grow up!"

I, too, laughed and poured tea into our dainty cups.

"What was your first career map, Pleasant?"

"College professor, teaching speech and English."

"You went to school and got degrees?"

"Been there, done that. Got the degrees and taught at three colleges for a total of six years."

"What happened?"

"It wasn't right for me. I wanted more."

Ida Rose smiled at my personal demonstration of her message. "The territory wasn't what you'd imagined, so you changed?"

"Drastically. Now I'm struggling to make a living as a storyteller."

"If you're going to evolve, you're required to make new maps based on what life throws at you. And,

Pleasant, I believe you'll make it."

## The universe doesn't forget.

The Sanskrit term akasha means "ether" or "sky." Several doctrines refer to *The Akashic Records* as the hall of human memories stored from the beginning of time. The library exists on the etheric plane, and many Eastern religions and philosophies make a note of the *Akasha*.

The *Bible* refers to the library as the Book of Life in both the Old Testament (Psalm 69:28) and the New Testament (Philippians 4:3, Revelation 3:5).

Whatever you choose to call it, this compendium of all history and knowledge records the journey of every soul in each of its incarnations—all the choices, agreements, actions, successes, and failures.

Your soul gathered together with the souls of your current family and created contracts before your birth. The contracts allowed the potential of evolution in this life, not only for you, but your family as well. Imagine the complexity of the algorithm required to assimilate the significant memories of all the souls involved and calculate the best-case scenarios dependent on your free-will choices!

These contracts can cause family dramas and expose the core of our life journey. This question is legitimate: "Why in God's name would I have chosen this father, mother, sibling, or friend?" The flip side of the question is also fair: "Why would this father, mother, sibling, or friend have chosen me?"

As father and son in this life, our individual souls understood and accepted the potential to heal past debts—not only his, and my, karmic debts, but those involving our entire family.

You might think it unfair to arrive on earth and

join a specific birth family, one that you chose, without your memory of past actions and relationships, but it's a necessary part of evolution.

## Take what you want but pay for it.
## Everything has its price.

Ida Rose Barber, the archetypical wise old woman, provided me with the gift of knowledge and awareness of the consequences of the choices I make. I've learned that free will isn't free. Three questions must be answered in each transaction with the universe:

*What do I want?*
*Am I willing to pay the cost?*
*Is it worth the cost?*

You choose your career path and pay the cost with study, hard work, and a conscious commitment of thirty or more years of your life. Your religious and political beliefs have price tags, often called judgement. You might judge others as they judge you. You choose to compromise when you meet your life partner and settle in for the long haul. The decisions you face expand exponentially and never end. Do you want children? When? How many? Where will you live, in a fancy mansion or a log cabin in the woods? Will you send your kids to college? What about your grandchildren? Consider the magnitude of the emotional, financial, and life-changing costs involved in the single partnership contract.

Once you've made a choice—any choice—if you are willing to pay the cost, feel it's worth it, and accept the consequences of your actions, you will grow in consciousness, light, and life.

## The map is not the territory.

The map is belief. The territory is reality. As Alan

Watts said, "The menu is not the meal." Many of your core maps, created during the first seven years of life, sustain or inhibit happiness and evolutionary progress. If you were raised Christian and believe you're a sinner, shame may affect your reality. If your family, school, and friends encouraged pride in your heritage and disdain for those who are different than you, discrimination, hate, and fear may rule your life.

If you look closely and honestly at the reality of your life, you'll probably discover that part of your map conflicts with another person's map and creates a disturbance in both of your worlds. When you feel stressed, ask yourself these three questions:

*What isn't working in my current map?*

*What "should" is interfering?*

*What belief or prejudice must I relinquish to return to a state of calm?*

Pulling together requires a steep climb beyond rigid religious, political, and family traditions. You must break free of the belief that your maps are the "right" ones and others "should" conform to your wants and needs. You might have to rip apart your old maps, set fire to them, and roast marshmallows while surveying the horizon and contemplating the new map you'll draw with your expanded knowledge of the territory.

Lucy tore up her core map early in life. Her father altered part of his core map, though it took him several years to do it. Both my father and I eventually changed our core maps and even created new ones together.

Human evolution requires you to be willing to alter your outdated core maps and adapt them to the reality of here and now. Adaptions often result in breakage, but don't worry. "There's a crack in everything," poet Leonard Cohen said. "That's how the light gets in."

~ ~ ~

# Karma

## CHAPTER THREE

*No man
ever steps in
the same river twice.
It's not the same river,
and he's not the same man.*

~Heraclitus~

# The Dying Dog

## A True Tale from Chiang Mai, Thailand

AFTER MOVING MY WORLDLY GOODS into the Na-kornping Condominium in Chiang Mai, I headed out to fill my empty fridge. As I stepped into the elevator, a tall, thin, aging man greeted me.

"I haven't seen you here before," he said. "American?"

"Yes, I am."

"Me, too." He smiled and stuck out his hand. "Name's Monte."

"Pleasant. Nice to meet you."

"Ditto. Where are you goin'?"

"I need to find a nearby grocery store. I just moved in today."

"Then you should check out TOPS. Great selection and only a five-minute walk. I'll take you there."

As we shopped, I learned that Monte is an expat with a dozen years of living in Thailand notched in his belt. A retired educator, generous, and always polite.

On the way back to the condo, Monte asked, "What're you doin' this evening, Pleasant?"

"Nothing planned."

"How about stoppin' by my room at 6:30 for a drink? Afterward, I know of an excellent café close by."

"Sounds great. 6:30 it is." The conversations shared that night, and many that followed, confirmed I'd made a genuine friend.

One day in March, Monte and I walked to the Old City for lunch at a restaurant known for its Northern Thai chicken soup. It was a quaint place and Thai culture seemed to ooze out of the walls. As usual, we ordered and delved deep into a variety of subjects.

"What're you workin' on these days, Pleasant?"

"I'm writing about the nature of karma in everyday life."

"By karma, you mean doing good and getting it back? Doing bad and your life sucks? That kind of karma?"

"Exactly."

Monte set his beer down and leaned in. "Let me tell you a story."

Intrigued, I mirrored Monte and leaned in, too. "Please do." I couldn't help but think that my karma had brought me a good karma story at the perfect moment.

"This happened around ten or twelve years ago, soon after I moved here from Bali. Three of us old-fart expats lived in a wreck of a hotel near Tha Phae Gate in the Old City. Building's gone now and a good thing, too. Cheap dump. The kind of place where you check in and stay till they toss you out."

"Been there a few times myself... somewhere else." We clicked drink mugs as Monte got on with his story.

"Anyway, Toothpick Jim, an American, and Big Al from Canada, and I are sitting at our usual table on the hotel's veranda, late one morning—"

"Toothpick Jim?" I asked.

"He always had a damn toothpick in his mouth, and Al must've weighed 300 pounds. Always wore red suspenders. Called 'em braces."

"Got it. Go on."

"So, Toothpick and Al had been out drinkin' and carousin' the night before and hadn't been to bed yet. I'd come home early and gotten a good night's sleep. We order breakfast, and the guys are tellin' me about their adventures when we smell somethin' foul. Toothpick says, 'Jesus! What the hell is that?' and Big Al pipes in with 'Smells like the sewer, only worse!'

"An old dog limps in from the street, a medium-sized mongrel, one of those street dogs. We're totally amazed that he just keeps on coming, staggerin' right up onto our veranda. That dog might have been white-haired as a pup, but a rough life and mange had turned him dirty-gray. His left ear was nearly chewed off. His right eye seemed permanently closed and his other one looked rummy. He probably smelled our food before he saw us. Hey, Pleasant buddy, you're lookin' uncomfortable. Should I stop?"

"No, no, it's okay. I'm just imagining the dog and where karma might come in. Please continue!"

"Okay. You'll see. As this mutt gets closer to our table, Big Al scoots his chair back and nearly falls off. Jim spits his toothpick toward the beast, and I began yelling for Arman, the hotel owner, who sits at the check-in counter 24/7. He rushes out to the veranda in time to see the dog flop down, roll over, and just lie there, hardly breathing. Arman kneels down, squints into its half-open eye, pinches its nose, and says, 'Dog sick.' Thanks, Arman. We know that already. Then Big Al says, 'And he's making me sick. What can we do?' I remember a veterinarian's office a few blocks away and ask Arman to call him."

Monte had become completely immersed in the memory, gesturing wildly, and acting out the events. Our restaurant had transformed into the veranda in his mind. I was mesmerized by his story as it unfolded.

"Arman shakes his head and warns us that the 'vet costs much baht.' Eyes wide and palms up, I glance over at Toothpick and Al. They nod in agreement, and Al sighs, 'We'll pay.' It doesn't take long for the vet to show up, an older gentleman, smart dresser, medical bag in hand. He puts on a protective smock, yellow rubber gloves, and kneels down to examine his new patient. He seems to know what he's doing. After checking over his patient, the vet sighs, stands up, and addresses us like we're the mutt's family. 'Sorry to say, the dog is dying.' Toothpick looks like a ghost with no toothpick to comfort him. Maybe he's feelin' a little kinship with that sorry soul. 'That mutt's had it rough,' he says. 'Sure ya can't fix him up, doc?'

"The vet starts packing up his gear and mumbling, 'Cannot. Too far gone. No hope.' My friends and I have a brief chat and come to the same conclusion. 'Give him the silver bullet,' I tell the vet. 'Help him end it all. It's the least we can do.'

"The vet's face gets all serious and solemn. He lowers his voice to deliver the verdict. 'Cannot do. Might have been a general.' With that, he turns and leaves! The three of us are speechless... then amazed. The pathetic old mutt seems to understand that no help's coming to save him. He slowly raises his head from the tile floor, shoots us a sorrowful look, and struggles to his feet. We watch as he drags his matted tail off the veranda and disappears down the street."

Yanking myself back into the present moment, I asked in a whisper, "Where did he go?"

"I have no idea. And we never smelled or saw that dog again." Monte went quiet for a spell, and then laughed. "Ha! 'Might have been a general!' That's exactly what the vet said. A corrupt and despicable old general who sent young bucks to their death? If so, I guess he deserved nothing good, just his lifelong suffering. Now that's karma for you!"

~ ~ ~

# Revenge

## Denver, Colorado, September 1951

THE RECURRING NIGHTMARES FIRST EMERGED at age eight. Asleep in my single bed on Chase Street, I awoke screaming in the middle of the night… in the middle of this dream.

*I'm a lad of the same age, in ancient Mesopotamia, the cradle of civilization, 2,000 years before the birth of Christ. I'm scared and feel my bladder release. Warm urine splashes on my dusty bare feet. My father squeezes my hand and pulls me forward, one step at a time. I dig my feet into the sand and yell, "No, no! I don't want to…" I hear my mother's wails from somewhere below us.*

*We're in an enormous cave with a crescent-shaped entrance. The midday sun pours in, illuminating the interior. A slanted granite altar rises from the cave's gaping mouth where our enemy's high priests await, adorned in ceremonial robes and tall, black conical hats.*

*My father picks me up and holds me close to his strong chest. His heart is pounding. Tears stream down his cheeks and dampen his black beard. He takes another step forward. He is a defeated warrior and is being sacrificed with his male heir. Deafening victory cheers erupt from the crowd gathered below the entrance to the cave.*

*The high priests facing us hold sharp stone daggers to sever our jugular veins. Other conquered men and their sons, my friends and neighbors, are with us. We are led to our deaths, one family at a time.*

*The frenzied clamor from the crowd drowns out the cries from the doomed as my father takes another step forward and sets me down. He leans close to my ear and whispers his final words. "I'm sorry, my son."*

*He is dragged to the altar, and I watch him die.*

*The next moment two priests lift me onto the altar and lay me on my back with my neck exposed. Looking toward the sun, I see the blade flash downward. Screaming for all I'm worth, I jerk myself awake!*

Dad ran into my bedroom, flipped on the light, and saw I wasn't not hurt or in danger. "Jesus Christ! It's just a bad dream. Stop crying. I mean it! Stop crying, or I'll give you something to cry about!"

I stuffed my tears.

"Not another peep from this room tonight. I need my sleep, dammit." He flipped off the light and left.

A month later, the nightmare reappeared. Mom heard my screams and rushed into my bedroom. "Hush, hush, honey. Don't wake up your dad. It's just a bad dream. I'll stay here with you. Try to go back to sleep."

The dream tormented me again in two months, but I awoke without screaming or crying, a survival tactic to avoid my father during this difficult time in our household. My folks weren't getting along and often woke my brothers and me with loud, bitter, midnight arguments.

My brother Bob was a year older than me, and Roger, two years younger. It would have been easier on us if my parents had separated sooner than they did. Divorce was uncommon in Colorado during the 1950s and marked a failed family. Dad decided to move out in 1955 when I was twelve. The afternoon he packed up to leave, things got ugly. He planned to live with a friend, but return that night and sleep on the sofa.

Dad was a control freak, insecure, and profoundly jealous. He never allowed Mom to complete her high school education, to learn to drive, to smoke, or even look in the direction of another man.

Mom puffed on a cigarette in the entryway, antagonizing Dad with a display of independence. I stood nearby and offered no help as he loaded the Ford station-wagon with his clothing.

Outraged by Mom's cigarette, he fumed, "You bitch." Then he turned his anger on me. "Get my hunting knife, Jerry. The one I loaned you."

I was dumbfounded, and my jaw dropped half open. Dad had wrapped the knife in trout-themed paper and given that knife to me on my birthday.

"You're not much of a hunter, Son, but you're a good fisherman. You're old enough for a proper knife. It's sharp. Don't ever let me catch you fooling around with it."

"But you gave it to me."

"God damn it, quit whining and bring it here."

"You did, too!" Mom yelled. "You gave it to him last year on his birthday. Now get out!"

Dad exploded and slapped her, knocking the cigarette out of her mouth.

My heart turned to ice. I spoke with a voice that frightened me. "Leave. Don't come back tonight. If you do, I'll kill you. If you ever hit Mom again, I'll kill you."

"So, you're a tough guy now?" Dad sneered. He let out a derisive laugh, threw himself into the stationwagon, and drove away.

I lay awake most of that night with the razor-sharp knife under my pillow. Dad didn't return until the following afternoon. He said nothing about the knife, packed his remaining clothes, and left for good. Two months later, my parents signed the divorce papers.

Had Dad returned that terrible night, I might've tried to kill him. The coldness clouding my heart continued relentlessly for too many years. I despised my father, found fault with him at every turn, and often spoke my hatred aloud. Had I known the actual cost of my righteous anger, I could've saved myself an abundance of pain.

## San Diego, California, March 1983

In the early 1980s, my storytelling and writing career landed me in San Diego where I met Stephanie, a professional breath-worker. She specialized in Rebirthing, a controversial practice founded in the '70s by Leonard Orr. It's ultimate goal is to re-experience one's actual birth in this lifetime and can be used to purge traumatic childhood memories.

I was in my early forties and worked with Stephanie for a year-long tutelage, focusing on what I found difficult in life. I also wanted to discover the impact of a childhood accident in which I suffered third-degree burns over thirty percent of my body, especially on my legs and buttocks. Skin grafts do not grow with the body, so I endured three subsequent operations from the age of four through twelve. After each surgery, I had to learn to walk again. Often challenged by gravity, I wanted balance in my physical as well as my emotional life. After several months of practicing "connected breathing," Stephanie invited me to attend a professional breath seminar.

"But I'm not a professional."

"You'll be my client, Pleasant, for a demonstration in front of the group."

When her turn came, she guided me with the familiar circular breath form, and I connected my inhale to my exhale without effort. Within ten minutes, I began to relive the nightmare of my youth as I became the boy in the cave about to be ritually sacrificed. I didn't enter into a dream. Unifying my breath with my eyes closed, I lay on a futon surrounded by nine adults. Fully aware, I explained what was happening using a few words. "I'm moving closer to the altar. They're laying me onto the killing slab."

"Stay with it," Stephanie whispered, "wherever it takes you."

*Sweat soaked through my clothing. The serpentine blade gleamed in the sunlight. I looked into the ebony eyes of my slayer, the high priest, and with a shock, recognized he was my father in my present life.*

"Oh, my!"

"You okay, Pleasant?"

I nodded yes.

"We're here with you. You're safe."

*Peering into Dad's compelling eyes, I witnessed a series of past life experiences. At first I saw myself as a handsome Roman boy of fourteen. I sang beautifully and showed promise as a poet. Sacked by the Greek army, our prov-*

*ince experienced many deaths. In that past life, Dad was a rough and cruel Greek warrior, and claimed me as his slave. I became his boy whore who he shared with his comrades. I wanted to kill him. A single flash of awareness revealed the entire story. After abusing me for three years, he choked me to death with his calloused hands.*

*Suddenly I was in Egypt, a middle-aged priest working in a private enclave in a pyramid. Papyrus scrolls were piled on a table in front of me. A soldier entered my chamber, and I realized this man was also my father, humbly seeking insight and guidance. Smug in my judgment, I gave him only a morsel, far less than he deserved.*

*The setting switched to the time of the Tang Dynasty in Imperial China. Dad and I were brothers, and as the eldest, he was allowed to marry first. He chose my beloved woman and laughed at me on his wedding day. My hatred lasted through that life and beyond.*

*In the next dream scene, I got my revenge. Queen Victoria ruled in England. I wore a powdered white wig and a black judge's robe in Her Majesty's Courts. Dad was brought before me on charges of petty thievery. Even though he had a large hungry family, I delighted in sentencing him to a lengthy prison term.*

A clear karmic pattern of revenge had become evident. We harmed each other with intent, again and again. The weight of our shared karma accumulated over centuries affected the balance of father and son in this life.

Stephanie slowly coaxed me back to the here and now. Twenty-five minutes had elapsed. I sat up and asked for water.

"What did you learn?" she asked, handing me a cup.

"The man who ended my life in Mesopotamia gave me life in this incarnation."

Who was the man that fathered me? The dad with three boys, two of which made him proud? The dad who repeatedly told me, "Don't be a pansy," and had humiliated me for years?

Dad excelled as an athlete and was a state champion wrestler in high school. He also played varsity football and expected nothing less from his boys. Bob and Roger didn't let him down, but I couldn't play contact sports due to my skin grafts.

I did participate in track and field in junior high, and joined the cross country team in high school. We won the Colorado State Championship for our division during my junior year. I wore my letter jacket to school every day of my senior year. Dad, who helped coach my brother's wrestling teams, never *once* watched me run.

Dad also took issue with my overabundant imagination before the age of nine. Due to the lack of books, art, and music at home, I'd create more appealing realities and be lost in my make-believe world for an hour or two. Dad berated me time and again whenever he caught me daydreaming. Misbehaving children got spanked in the 1950s, and Dad was an equal opportunity disciplinarian. My brothers and I routinely felt the sting of his belt.

I'll never forget two of his oft-repeated quotes as I grew up.

"Do as I say, not as I do."

"They may not love me, but by God, they'll respect me."

At times he could be kind. I recall a little clown doll he bought for me when the measles took me down. Dad made certain he outfitted his boys for hunting and fishing. When we were quite young, he carried us across a swift running Colorado river. The frigid water came up to his thighs, and the rocks below were slippery. First he took Bob in his arms, maneuvered the river's rapids slowly, carefully, and set him down on the other bank. Then he waded back across to get Roger and me. I stood shaking on the shore.

He smiled and reassured us. "Don't worry boys. I won't drop you." With both of us hugging him, he crossed the river for the third time. "Hang on tight. I've got you."

We felt safe in his strong arms.

As a child, I didn't realize how hard he worked as a carpenter, or how difficult it was to keep a family fed, clothed, and sheltered. Stress intensified daily in our household until the end of each month when the funds were low and the milk bill due.

At the time of the regression experience, Dad had been out of my life in any meaningful way for twenty-four years. I'd come out as a gay man in my late twenties to everyone in my family but him. He *knew*, but that was a topic never discussed. I lived in Seattle, then San Diego, and back to Seattle during those years. He and his second wife, Rose, stayed in Denver. We'd have a telephone conversation every few months and discuss nothing of importance. Dad wasn't interested in my adult life or storytelling career. Most certainly, he didn't ask about my relationships. A perfunctory "Love you, Son" and "Love you too, Dad" ended each call.

The big question emerged. How do I heal our karmic relationship? I couldn't invite Dad over for a conversation. We lived too far apart. Nor could I call him for an in-depth discussion on what I'd discovered. He'd never believe me, and I couldn't blame him. I had to tackle the situation on my own.

Each morning as I sat to meditate, I focused on a clear intention.

*I wish to heal the relationship with my father.*

Anger flared up throughout the meditations. I nearly gave up after the first month. I altered my intention.

*I forgive my father.*

My anger continued to fester from a legacy of too many put-downs and too much pain. How could I possibly forgive him? A month later, I altered my intention again.

*I forgive myself.*

Anger grew less. Each time it resurfaced, I surrendered, breathed rhythmically, and silently repeated a new mantra.

*I forgive the past. The battle is over. Thank you, God, and so it is.*

Slowly but surely, my deepest emotions shifted from anger to relief, and finally, acceptance. Eight months of conscious effort changed my everyday life and relationships. The depressing weight of judgment lifted from my physical, emotional, and spiritual self. My cold heart melted. I began smiling at life and seeing more possibilities for my evolution as a human being, being human. I became a much happier man.


## Denver, Colorado, December 1983

I enjoyed traveling to Denver to spend Christmas with my close-knit family—Mom, my stepdad, siblings, and their families. I did not look forward to the annual visit with Dad and his wife.

The latest winter fashion for gays was a colorful scarf wrapped twice around the neck, which flowed down the front of the coat, all the way to the knee. Mom bought me two identical scarves and sewed them together.

Wearing a heavy, wool pea coat, matching navy-blue watch cap, and the red-and-yellow scarf, the gay son arrived at Dad's apartment bearing brightly wrapped gifts—just in time for dinner.

As Dad opened the door, I sensed something amiss. I said hello and handed Rose the gifts. Although a handshake was Dad's style, I hugged him. He didn't hug me back. He took my coat to the hall closet. Rose asked about my flight. Before I could answer her, Dad exploded with anger.

"If you ever do *anything* to harm the DeSpain name," he threatened with menace and a raised fist, "I'll follow to the ends of the earth, and *I will kill you!*"

His unbridled rage came out of nowhere. We hadn't argued in years. Dad's ancient warrior-self must have recognized a shift in our fundamental relationship, and he was infuriated.

Rose retreated to the kitchen.

My first reaction was to grab my coat and bolt out the door. My second thought was to fight back with harsh words. Instead I took a deep breath and asked an obvious question. "You're angry with me, right?"

"You'll never know how mad I am. I want to hit you." He shook his fist in front of my face. "With this fist!"

I took another full breath. Words came to me without forethought. "You're right, Dad. I've been an imperfect son. I want you to... no... I ask you to forgive me."

Taken aback, he stared at me with eyes full of doubt and confusion. His fist opened and his arm fell.

Rose crept back into the hallway. "Enough, you two! Please, let's sit at the table and eat a nice meal."

Without responding, Dad turned, marched into his bedroom, and closed the door. He emerged in ten interminable minutes and took his position at the head of the table. He neither looked at me nor spoke.

I sat on the right side, across from Rose. We filled our plates with pasta, sausage, and salad, and began to eat. A minute later, Dad picked up his dinner knife with his right hand. He pointed the blade at me and his knuckles became white. With a strong will, he lowered the knife back to the table and purposely turned the blade inward toward his plate. He raised his wet eyes to mine. "Son," he said, his voice breaking, "I've been an imperfect father. I want you to forgive me."

I nodded yes and began to weep. Dad cried. Rose cried.

The war ended, and our relationship forever changed. Whereas I'd had months to prepare, Dad hadn't known another choice would present itself upon my arrival at his door. His warrior-self rose to defend his honor, his past, his present, and I was proud of him.

During the ensuing years, we spoke on the phone once each month. After discussing declining health matters, weather conditions, or football scores, Dad would ask about me, about my career, about my real life. Many times our conversations finished with warmhearted feelings from Dad. "I'm proud of you, Son. I love you."

Robert Alan DeSpain died in the year 2000 at age 77. I spoke loving words at his funeral.

~ ~ ~

# The Shadow Knows

"WHO KNOWS WHAT EVIL LURKS in the hearts of men?" (And women?) "The Shadow knows!" The opening line of the popular radio show scared me when I was nine years old. The eerie voice implied that everyone had a dark side. I didn't want a dark side. I'd learned that evil was wrong on all counts.

In Jungian philosophy, the Shadow is an archetype, an unconscious aspect of personality that everyone carries. We tend to keep it hidden, especially from ourselves. Accepting your sinister side is required if you're prepared to forge a path to freedom from the karmic weight of your past and current negative actions.

A few years ago, I spent several weeks in Nong Khai, Thailand, a small city on the Mekong River. Visiting a local temple, I discovered a quiet alcove in the main hall, and sat on a cushion. I closed my eyes and began to meditate. After ten minutes, I felt a presence nearby. Opening one eye, I was shocked to see the "hulk" attired in a saffron-colored robe! Without forethought, I blurted in a whisper, "How'd you get to be so big?"

The monk tossed back his head and laughed. "I was a Mui Thai boxer as a youth. I had to grow strong to survive."

"You speak English very well."

"I learned in school. My name is Wan."

"Nice to meet you. I'm Pleasant."

"Indeed, you are! Well, Pleasant, would you like to chat?"

"I'd love to."

Wan walked me across the cool, tiled floor to a further alcove, one adorned with a golden statue of Buddha. "We'll talk here."

We sat facing one another. He reminded me of a kind headmaster at school. Soft, brown eyes revealed intelligence, and hard-earned wrinkles told of worldly experience. "When did you become a monk?" I asked.

"Thirty years ago."

"And it's been good?"

With a quick nod, Wan smiled. "I've found peace, and that's good. What brings you here today?"

"Frustration. The news is filled with cancer, wars, and death. It isn't fair that so many suffer."

"Yes," he agreed. "It has always been so."

"But *why*? Why does it continue?"

"We fail to see the darkness within ourselves. Instead, we find evil in others to justify killing. The Buddha said, 'All those alive have their karma. It's our inheritance. Karma separates us into low and high states and keeps the struggle alive.'"

"Our inheritance?" I asked. "What do you mean by that?"

"We came into this life with the weight of past actions. It creates our journey into more light or more dark."

"Can we ever change karma?"

"Yes, but it takes many lives. You must grow your spirit in each one."

"Grow my spirit?"

"Do right action. Do less harm."

Wan reached over, gently took my hand, and tied a thin, red, cotton string around my wrist. "This is for protection and good fortune. Wear it for three days." He unfolded his thick legs and stood, towering over me. "I'm sorry but I must go. The walkways will not get swept with words."

For years I'd kept my Shadow under wraps, embedded in my judgmental personality. I'd grown comfortable with the coldness at the core of my heart. Treating my father like an unlovable relative, I justified keeping my distance by stuffing *my* feelings and naming *his* faults.

No one told me I carried a heavy karmic weight with every step I took. No one explained I had to examine my dark-side if I wanted to lighten up. No one shared that to move forward with my evolution, I had to embrace more than my ego-self. I had to embrace *all* of me.

Shadow and karma are interrelated and fundamental to being human. You can deny them, but you can't escape them. Most people use a defense mechanism to cope on a daily basis. Carl Jung called it *projection*. You project on to others that which you abhor in yourself. You blame others instead of blaming yourself. Your ego says, "*You* are right, and *they* are wrong." Most of what we project is fear, the evil that lurks in our hearts.

On a visit to my former home in Troy, New York, a local realtor asked to sit at my table in a crowded café. As we were discussing our respective careers, he asked me to define the word karma.

I gave him a simple answer. "It's a Sanskrit term describing the law of consequences."

"Well, I'm Catholic, so I don't believe in karma."

"Certainly your choice, but karma believes in you."

You can call the Law of Karma whatever you like. Call it the Law of Attraction: "If you focus on positive or negative thoughts, you can bring positive or negative experiences into your life." Or get scientific and call it Newton's Third Law of Motion: "For every action in nature, there is an equal and opposite reaction." Or call on a quote from the New Testament: "As you sow, so shall you reap." Whether you are Western or Eastern, Catholic or Buddhist, Atheist or Agnostic, the law applies to you, to everyone. Your Shadow knows that what you put forward in the universe returns to you. You created your Shadow, and only you can heal what you've created.

Healing your karma starts with accepting that you've lived several lives, all of which contributed to the struggles and joys in this life. The renowned author and mythology professor Joseph Campbell said, "The cave you fear to enter holds the treasure you seek." The treasure you seek is freedom from past action. Freedom means forgiveness. The source of forgiveness is yourself.

The first conscious *step* in your healing is to be honest about family relationships. With whom do you have conflict? Don't list your reasons for the conflict. Reasons tend to be projections, and your family member's reasons are as valid as yours. Do you feel the coldness within your heart? Do not, for any reason, involve your relatives in the process. You must walk this path alone. You cannot heal another.

I hadn't met a "wise man or woman" with the knowledge to help me accomplish this type of healing. I simply focused on my desire and trusted my guardians for guidance. The eight months needed to forgive and accept my whole-self were the most emotionally challenging time of my life. I resisted each day. Worthiness, my ego reminded me again and again, was beyond my grasp. Still, I stayed the course until the sludge began to shift.

By sharing my experience with you, I have faith it will inspire you and present a method of healing which worked for me. But it's your faith that will determine your success. You will know pain and joy. Acknowledge there is work ahead that only you can do. Do not worry; you are not alone. The Creator and your guardians are with you.

To begin, create a comfortable, quiet space where you will not be interrupted for ten minutes or more during the following meditation.

Sit comfortably in a chair with your back straight and feet on the floor. Close your eyes, calm your breath, and with clear intention, say three times:

*I'm here to heal. I forgive myself for the harm I've caused. Thank you, God. And so it is.*

*I'm here to heal. I forgive myself for the harm I've caused. Thank you, God. And so it is.*

*I'm here to heal. I forgive myself for the harm I've caused. Thank you, God. And so it is.*

Your Shadow will awaken, and a feeling of heaviness will appear. Your ego will probably say, "Forget about it! This is a waste of time." Overrule your ego. You have a mission to accomplish, and these initial steps are vital.

Focus on your breath. Create balance by slowly inhaling to the count of five and exhaling to the count of five, in and out three times. Then again say, three times:

*I'm here to heal. I forgive myself for the harm I've caused. Thank you, God. And so it is.*

*I'm here to heal. I forgive myself for the harm I've caused. Thank you, God. And so it is.*

*I'm here to heal. I forgive myself for the harm I've caused. Thank you, God. And so it is.*

Be brave. Do not fear the darkness as it descends. Welcome it. You are not alone. Feel the weight upon your shoulders and neck.

Straighten your back, balance your breath, and again, say three times,

*I'm here to heal. I forgive myself for the harm I've caused. Thank you, God. And so it is.*

*I'm here to heal. I forgive myself for the harm I've caused. Thank you, God. And so it is.*

*I'm here to heal. I forgive myself for the harm I've caused. Thank you, God. And so it is.*

What you feel is the truth, that which is so at that moment. Allow your feelings to flow. Resist the desire to escape with all your strength. You're in the heart of the cave—your heart. Search for a spark of light by again calming and balancing your breath. Say three times:

*I forgive you, (your first name), and I love you.*
*I forgive you, (your first name), and I love you.*
*I forgive you, (your first name), and I love you.*

Your ego might cry forth, "No, no, no. I'm not worthy." Resist. Overcome the temptation to quit. Be strong. Again, say three times:

*I forgive you, (your first name), and I love you.*
*I forgive you, (your first name), and I love you.*
*I forgive you, (your first name), and I love you.*

Ego will lessen. Calm and balance your breath, and now, with arms wrapped around your shoulders, say three final times:

*I forgive you, (your first name), and I love you.*
*I forgive you, (your first name), and I love you.*
*I forgive you, (your first name), and I love you.*

Relax, breathe deeply, and then say once:

*Thank you, God. And so it is.*

Your meditation is complete. Healing karma stimulates your heart. Lie down for five minutes, breathing, feeling, simply being, and then return to your daily life with a promise that you'll meditate again tomorrow, and the days to follow.

It may take a month, six months, or even a year until you feel the shift, the breaking up of darkness. The shift starts with a splinter, followed by a crack, and continues with a chunk of weight falling. The light of love and life fills the voids, step by step. The shift is noticeable in the difference you feel, day to day. The shift leads to moments of unexpected sadness and spontaneous hilarity. Your breath changes. You fill your lungs with ease. Former bodily aches and pains disappear. Overall, you experience peace within.

The root-cause of battles—*projection*—weakens. Finding fault with your world, family, friends, and neighbors takes a back seat to honestly being human, alive, and consciously taking an evolutionary journey.

Miraculously, you don't need details of all the harm you have caused in this life and past lives. The Universe remembers your actions and doesn't judge them. You do. You're in control. Thus, "I forgive myself…" You can't truly forgive another until you have forgiven yourself. You can't truly love another until you discover the love of your whole-self.

The ego must surrender in its battle with the heart. To "surrender" is not to give up, but to give in to what is so. Taking this meditative journey with humility and patience produces an awareness of your higher, wiser self. You are more than a human being, being human. You are spirit in action. Evolution is not only possible. It's probable… and inevitable.

A follower once asked Buddha, "When is the right time to become enlightened?"

"Now," is all he said.

The answer is always now. The answer is the same for healing. And the rest of your life begins now.

~ ~ ~

# Nature

## CHAPTER FOUR

*In all things of nature
there is something
of the marvelous.*

~Aristotle~

# The Boy Who Drew Cats

## Japan

IN THE DAYS OF OLD, A BOY WAS BORN into a family of impoverished rice farmers living outside a tidy village in Japan. They named the small and sickly baby Hong, which means wild swan. As he aged, Hong failed to develop into a robust youth like his brothers and sisters.

One evening after all the children had gone to sleep, Hong's father shook his head and said to his wife, "He'll never be able to do his share of work."

"You're right," she sighed. "We must take him to the temple. He might make a better priest than a farmer."

At the tender age of ten, Hong became an apprentice at the local Shinto temple. He learned his lessons, swept the cold stone floors, and washed the saffron-colored robes of the priests. He weeded vegetable gardens each day and lit the temple candles each night. Studying hard each afternoon, Hong learned to write on rice paper with a fine brush and black ink.

One day, with just a few strokes of his brush, Hong drew a cat. His jet-black eyes burned under his brow as presented the artwork to his teacher.

"You have talent," the old priest said. "I want you to practice drawing pictures every day." He grinned with a quick wink. "Along with your other lessons."

Hong discovered that he loved to draw and paint pictures. He drew temple buildings and the faces of the priests. He painted village children and stray dogs. Most of all, he practiced drawing cats—large cats and small ones, young cats and old ones, cats at play and at rest, fighting cats and hunting cats. They shimmered with life and seemed ready to leap from the page.

When he turned fourteen, the priests made a difficult decision and instructed the teacher to break the news. "You are blessed with a unique talent," the old priest told Hong. "We feel that you'll be a better artist than a priest. I'm sorry to say that you must leave this temple and make your way in the world."

Hong felt sad upon hearing this news. He had nowhere to go. He couldn't return to his family as a failed priest because it would bring shame upon them. He had only himself and his talent, so he gathered his art supplies, hitched up his robe, and began a random journey through the countryside. He drew pictures of farms and families, animals and buildings, and earned enough to survive while wearing out his sandals along the way. With no family, no home, and the constant bittersweet memory of new friends left behind, he was lonely to his core.

Late one afternoon as Hong climbed a steep mountain path, a fierce rain squall nearly washed him off the ridge. He crawled beneath a rocky ledge and waited for the storm to pass.

Soon an old hermit, skin and bones dressed in drenched rags, stumbled up the path and spied Hong hunched under the ledge. "I beg you, young one, may

I share your shelter with you?"

"Yes, grandfather, of course!" Hong hopped up and helped the hermit remove the tattered satchel from his stooped shoulder. "You are welcome to this rock and my meal. It's not much, but I've got a piece of dried fish and one rice ball. I'll give you half."

"Thank you so much, my son." Impressed by Hong's generosity, the hermit devoured the food and listened intently as Hong spilled out the story of his trials.

Hong's tale wove from his early childhood to that moment sitting with the hermit. He laced his fingers together behind his neck, leaned back on the rough rocks, and gazed into the darkness beyond the ledge. "You know, grandfather, I think the Creator of All Things put me on the earth to draw."

"I believe you, lad." The hermit paused and stroked his wispy white beard. "I feel you have found yourself on the right path. An ancient temple rests at the top of this mountain. Go there. The priests need your talent."

After a night huddled together to ward off the fury of nature, they parted ways the next morning. The hermit bowed in thanks and headed down to the valley. Hong set his sights up the mountain. When Hong arrived at the temple as the sun bowed to kiss the horizon, the massive stone building was eerily silent. No chanting came from inside. No birds sang in the nearby trees. The air was still, the leaves motionless like one of his paintings.

This is not like any temple I have ever seen, Hong thought. It feels more like a tomb than a temple. He summoned his courage, approached the formidable door, and knocked. Hong stepped back and stood like a statue for an infinite minute. No one answered.

He knocked harder, longer. The heavy oaken door remained closed.

"Is anyone there?" he hollered at the door. "I'll work for food and shelter!"

Still no answer.

Hong paced around the temple until he found a massive tree, felled by the storm, resting against the wall. One branch led to a high window. He scampered up the trunk, dragged his body up the branch to the open window, and lowered himself into the temple's main room. The final rays of sunlight peeking through the narrow windows were fading to black. Hong used his flint stone to light a candle. A thick layer of dust carpeted the expansive, nearly empty room. A white, silk, three-panel screen stood in one corner. He examined it closely. No marks, decorations, or pictures adorned either side of the panels. A perfect canvas awaiting the master's brush, Hong thought.

He retrieved his art supplies from his pack and began to draw. His hand floated across the silk like a feather on a summer breeze. Cats flowed from the depths of his soul, down the muscles in his arm, through the bristles of the brush onto his makeshift canvas—big cats and little ones, wild and tame, leopard cats peering through forest foliage, fat house cats on doorsteps, cats tumbling in play, cats languid in sleep, cats in every position he could imagine. When he'd covered each panel, front and back, from top to bottom and side to side, Hong plopped down on the floor to admire his work. The cats looked alive. He thought he heard them purr.

Tucking his cherished brush and ink bottle in the folds of his robe, he yawned and spoke to his cats. "I am so tired. I think I could sleep for a week."

He found a vacant alcove in a nearby room, snuffed out his candle, and dropped into a deep sleep. It was the worst night of his young life. Horrible dreams tormented Hong for hours, nightmares filled with screaming, fighting and blood.

At long last, Hong awakened to the sound of birds singing for the new day. Rubbing his eyes, he shuffled into the main room. His breath stopped at the scene in front of him. Convinced the nightmare continued to haunt him, he rubbed his eyes again.

In the center of the room lay a rat the size of a 300-pound bear with a long black tail snaking across the floor. Yellow-brown razor teeth protruded from its pointed snout. Hong leapt back against the wall, but the rat did not move. Inching closer to the rat, Hong thought it must be either asleep, or, he hoped, dead. He tapped it once with his bare foot. The rat stayed still. Dead, thank god. As Hong bent down for a closer examination, he saw the open scars covering the body, as if it had been shredded by samurai swords. Hong's eyes swung from the rat to the screen. Vivid red blood dripped from the jaws and claws of every single cat he had created.

Hong jerked around as the main temple door creaked open, and a shaved head slowly appeared behind it. Wide-eyed, the head stared at the rat. Then at the screen. Then at Hong. "Who are you?"

"I'm Hong," he stammered. "Last night I knocked but—"

"Why are you here?" the head demanded.

"I just needed shelter… and the tree branch—"

"Did you kill the demon?"

"No, no. I just painted your screens. I'm sorry. Then I went to sleep."

The head stared silently for a few seconds as its eyes darted around the room. Then it disappeared, and the door closed. Hong held his breath as he looked back at the screen. He didn't remember drawing the slight smile on the leopard's face.

Again the door creaked open, and one by one, cautiously, ten priests filed into the room. One by one, they each bowed low before Hong.

The final priest, the elder, stepped forward and bowed even lower. "Young Hong-san, thank you, thank you, thank you. You have saved us from the demon rat which has haunted and harassed us for months."

Still in a mild state of shock, Hong didn't know what to say, so he just nodded and listened.

The priest spread his arms as his lips spread into a kind smile. "You are forever welcome here at this temple. Please join our family and be our resident artist. You belong with us."

Hong stayed. He'd finally found his purpose, his place, and his family. He drew and painted each day and became known as one of Japan's greatest artists. He drew until he was too old and shaky to create the cats he envisioned. Then he painted in his mind and in his heart. When Hong's time arrived to leave this world, his ashes—along with his trusty brush and favorite ink bottle he'd used to paint the screens so long before—were buried in the temple's courtyard.

~ ~ ~

# The Guru

## Seattle, Washington, July 1973

ONE FRIDAY AFTERNOON ON THE DECK of his house boat moored on Lake Union, I sat enjoying a delicious lunch with a beautiful African-American friend named John. At thirty years of age, he was two years older, two inches taller, and two shades darker than me. And more adventurous.

"Want to meet a living saint?" he asked with that usual twinkle in his eye.

"Is Mother Theresa in town?"

"I'm serious. An Indian guru named Swami Muktananda is visiting Seattle. He's staying in a mansion on Capitol Hill and there's an open house tomorrow at 1 p.m."

"You're going?" I asked.

"I am. It's bound to be interesting."

"All right. I'll pick you up at 12:30."

The Seattle Transcendental Meditation Center had opened a year earlier, and I'd signed up. Meditating for twenty minutes, twice each day, had provided genuine results. I experienced calm at the center, slept better, and had more energy. Settling into my meditation that Saturday morning, I silently repeated my mantra, meaningless sounding words which contained subtle vibrations, and quickly melted into a blissful state. Normally, it would take ten or more minutes to realize any type of transcendence. That experience proved to be the beginning of a most unusual day.

Driving to Capitol Hill with John, I asked, "So what makes this guy a saint?"

"He can awaken cosmic energy in others."

"Awaken cosmic energy? What does that mean?"

"Sometimes you feel bliss during your meditations, right?"

"Yes."

"Well, he can make it happen for someone with just a thought, a touch, or a look. At least that's what I've heard."

This swami was beginning to intrigue me. "And where's he from?"

"Bangalore, the southwestern region of India."

"How old do you think he is?"

"No idea," John answered. "They say he's ageless."

Parking my car near the mansion proved impossible due to the number of vehicles jamming the streets, but John had a solution. "There's a lot about ten blocks from here. We can walk."

Arriving at the mansion, we realized the event had already started. A hand-written whiteboard sign was posted on the impressive wooden doors.

> Meet Swami Muktananda.
> Open House noon to 3 p.m.
> Please remove shoes before entering.

A sea of shoes and sandals stretched across the wide portico. We added our footwear to the mix, passed through the arched foyer, and entered the largest room I'd ever seen in a private home. Two hundred or more people sat quietly on the marble floor in orderly rows, facing a dais. Wearing a saffron-colored robe and an orange woolen cap, Muktananda rested in a high-backed, regally carved, wooden chair.

The women sat on the left side of the room, the men on the right. A broad center aisle separated the sexes. No one spoke. They just gazed at the guru. A feeling of serenity along with a whiff of sandalwood permeated the air.

Standing alongside us at the back of the room, a barefoot American man swathed in an orange robe, smiled and said, "You are welcome here. Would you like to meet Baba?"

"Baba?" I asked. "Who's Baba?"

"Muktananda," John whispered. "It's what his followers call him."

"Yes," said our guide. "It's a nickname for Father."

"I'd love to meet him."

"Me, too," said John.

Our guide led us up the center aisle to stand, face to face, with the guru, who slowly opened his eyes and greeted us with a gentle smile. I was instantly charmed.

Muktananda didn't speak much English and communicated through an interpreter. John was introduced, and after a brief exchange, our guide led him to the back of the hall to sit with the other late arrivals.

My turn came to meet the master. His deeply lined, nut-brown face displayed a hard-earned age, which I guessed to be around 70. His black eyes, hooded by heavy brows and softened by his smile, penetrated my very being.

"I'm honored to meet you," I said. "My name is Pleasant."

Upon hearing my unusual moniker, Baba's expression shifted from beatific to curious. "Where did you get your name?"

With the interpreter's help, I explained my roots in the American South and my status as the fifth generation "Pleasant" in my family.

"And your work?" Baba asked.

"I tell stories."

He laughed aloud, and then said, "I love stories. What kind do you tell?"

"All kinds—folk and fairy tales, myths, legends, true stories, and the occasional Zen tale."

We conversed for five minutes while the people on the floor remained patient. Three other visitors waited behind me. Muktananda paid them no mind and gave me his full attention.

"Do you meditate?" he asked.

"Yes, I do. I practice Transcendental Meditation."

"Ah! Maharishi Mahesh Yogi, a good man."

Smiling in agreement, I turned to the interpreter. "Please tell Baba that I have a gift for him."

I removed a prized stone from my pocket, the size of a nickel, but oval-shaped and adobe brown. I hadn't planned on giving it away, but happily handed to the powerful man sitting before me.

Muktananda received it with gentleness. After examining both sides of the stone, he asked several questions. "Where did you get it?"

"I'd found it last year on the banks of the Skagit River in Washington."

"What does it mean to you?"

"It's my secret charm." I felt like a proud school boy during Show and Tell. "See, it has the symbol of infinity on it, white and etched by nature." I flipped it over in his hand. "And the other side is perfectly smooth."

"Hmm. Very beautiful. Do you always carry it with you?"

"Always."

"Do you love it?" he asked.

"Yes."

Wrapping his fingers tightly around it and holding his hand to his heart, he said, "I love it as well."

Breathing deeply, he closed his eyes for several seconds, then spoke through the interpreter who said, "Baba has a gift for you."

And the master placed the stone in my hand.

I had a flash of awareness. By accepting the talisman and imbuing it with his essence, Baba had given me, in return, a greater gift. It wasn't the object that mattered, but rather, the giving and receiving.

Muktananda saw that I understood and smiled.

My heart seemed to expand in my chest. I nodded my thanks and turned to leave the dais, but the interpreter said, "Wait."

I spun back. Baba pointed to a space on the floor in the first row, directly to his left.

"Baba would like you to sit here, near him."

I sat.

The remaining visitors were introduced and then directed to the back. During the next group ceremony, Muktananda spoke briefly before leading us in fifteen minutes of spirited chanting. Then, eyes closed, we meditated for a brief time.

The interpreter explained that Baba needed to rest and asked us to return in an hour for the lecture on consciousness followed by a question and answer session. Everyone rose to leave, and I found John in the crowd talking with friends.

"You staying for the rest of it?" he asked.

"Yes."

"Okay. I'll get a ride with these guys."

"Great. And John, thanks for inviting me here."

"Muktananda seems to like you."

"It's mutual."

As John left with his friends, the interpreter approached and motioned me to a quiet corner. "Would you like a private audience with Baba?"

Taken by surprise, I muttered, "Sure. But what does one do in a private audience?"

As he led me by the arm to the upstairs library, he gave me some simple advice "Ask... for what you want."

The oak paneled room, resplendent with floor-to-ceiling bookshelves displaying thousands of hardbound tomes, whispered tranquility. Four other guests—three women and one man—were already seated at an elegant table. I joined them, and we remained silent awaiting the guru.

A few moments later, Baba arrived. After his interpreter had closed the library doors, the master sat in the single chair in a divinely lit alcove on the far side of the room. He closed his eyes and remained perfectly still.

Matching my breath to his, I felt my heartbeat slow. Warmth enfolded me. I felt loved.

Muktananda opened his eyes, and with his orange-robed arm, motioned me over to his chair. I kneeled before him on the plush wool rug. After scrutinizing me with profound intensity, he nodded to the interpreter at his side.

"What is it you seek?" came the question.

"I want to see and gain understanding," I said.

Not waiting for the translation, the master leaned forward and touched my forehead on the ridge between my eyes with his thumb. He applied a light, twisting pressure, then released me.

A warm vibration infused my lower spine, traveling up to my heart and beyond. I looked into Baba's eyes, and he nodded affirmatively. The interpreter asked me to return to my seat at the table. While waiting as the others individually held court with the guru, I lost all sense of time.

(I learned later that the technique, called *Chaktipat*, is used to open the third eye.)

The library doors opened, and another helper announced that the lecture was about to begin. Baba whispered to his interpreter and pointed to me. The other four visitors filed out and walked down the stairs to sit in the crowded main room. I was told to stay and watch the proceedings from the balcony.

Muktananda, again seated in his chair on the dais,

swept his eyes over the entire audience, then glanced up to me. He smiled and nodded, as if to say, "Pay close attention."

His silent command was unnecessary. I couldn't take my eyes off him and the crowded room. I could *see*!

Effused with golden light, the guru gestured with his right arm and a cascade of energy enveloped the entire room. He launched into a story, then paused and laughed as a myriad of light tumbled, flowed, and danced.

Still separated with women on the left and men on the right, the people crowded together on the floor, showered in colors. I saw greens, yellows, blues, purples, and even a few reds. Whenever a connection was made between the teller and the listeners, the colors conjoined. Muktananda commanded the focal point of all the bright swirling ethers.

Suddenly an older man in the back of the room leaped to his feet and yelled, "You're nothing but a fake, Muktananda, like all gurus!"

Angry red energy flew over the heads of the audience and encircled the master. Baba stopped his story, stared directly at the disrupter, and surprised everyone by laughing long and loud. A powerful golden light swallowed the red vibrations, floated to the back of the room, and enveloped the irate man. Momentarily dumbfounded, he too laughed, sat down on the floor, and said, "I feel like a fool!"

The crowd roared! The swirls of hues and emotions intensified. The master looked up at me with a wide grin.

I intuitively understood that light and color emanate from each of us, all the time. The men offered blues and purples; the women offered greens and yellows. Individually, each person effused unique mixtures of color. The master easily flooded the space with golden light. I witnessed how we communicate with more than thoughts, words, and stories. We share light-energy each time we speak, each time we listen.

An hour later, Muktananda ended the gathering by leading a group chant. He looked up at me sitting on the balcony above, one last time.

I mouthed, "Thank you."

When the time came to leave, I gathered my wits the best I could, and headed down the stairs. Intercepting me, the young interpreter motioned me to the same corner as before.

"Baba invites you to join us."

"Join you?"

"Be one of us. Live and travel with us. Become enlightened with us."

I paused to consider, but the answers came immediately. My heart, full of love for the master, said yes. My head, full of logic and reason, said no. "Thank you for your kind offer. Even though I would love the opportunity, please tell Baba that this just isn't the time for me to commit to a master. I must follow the path I've begun to travel. And please, please thank him for the many gifts bestowed on me during this incredible day."

"If you change your mind, you can join us in Portland, Oregon. We'll be there all next week!"

I walked outside and located my shoes. The late afternoon, French-blue, summer sky sparkled. After retrieving my car from the parking lot, I drove to the city arboretum and parked. The moment I stepped out, I felt the trees, grass, and abundant flowers calling me. I became intimately involved with my lush surroundings as I strolled down a shaded pathway. I was alone, yet not alone. In a grove of tall Douglas firs, I felt the trees emitting a slow, steady vibration. I felt the faint flow of energy connecting to my life force. Tears fell from my eyes, and I heard myself say, "Yes," and again, "Yes."

I drove home and collapsed on my sofa. Without warning, and from both sides of my forehead, I felt as if sliding door had shut. My third eye closed and the subtle vision ceased. My nervous system lacked sufficient strength to sustain the experience.

Two days later, my third eye reopened for eleven hours. The following week, I cherished a fifteen-hour stretch. Later that month, I saw for a day and a night. Then it was over, or so I thought.

For several months, I realized that my intuitive sight remained partially intact, as it does to this day. I'm often aware of the auras around others, most often while discussing human consciousness.

I continue to carry the infinity stone, my talisman, a precious gift from the guru.

~ ~ ~

# Learning to See

*I declare this world is so beautiful*
*that I can hardly believe it exists.*
~Ralph Waldo Emerson~

I AM GAZING AT THE SEA AND WRITING about learning to see. The balcony of my rented condo overlooks the Gulf of Thailand which stretches around Cambodia and Vietnam into the Pacific Ocean.

As the sun rises, gray-green waves gently break on

the sand, seventeen floors below. Small but constant, the dancing white-capped waves linger on the shore, slip back into the sea, and make room for more. A Thai man and woman hold hands and stroll along the shoreline as the cool water washes their bare feet.

I feel a humid breeze caressing my skin. I inhale the sea-scented air and taste a hint of salt on my tongue. As I write, my ears pick up the purr of three fishing trawlers in the distance, trudging across the bay in search of schools of fish they can't see.

Nature has awakened my senses, and I'm "seeing" with all of them.

The word "see" has many meanings. You see the stars. You see what you can do about a problem. You see red. You see eye to eye. You plan to see someone tomorrow. You see into the future. You see if it matters to you. See what I mean?

Humans have come a long way since the beginning when they could only see as far as the horizon of the nature surrounding them. These days you have glasses to improve your vision. On television or the internet, you can see life on the other side of the planet—while it's happening. You can look down onto Earth from a satellite. You can see millions of miles into the universe with the aid of telescopes, space voyagers, and radio waves. You can see inside yourself with electron microscopes and x-ray machines.

But *what* do you see? *Things. Or matter.* Animal, mineral or vegetable maybe, but all are things, matter made of "real" stuff—elements, molecules, atoms, gases, liquids and solids. The *Oxford Living Dictionary* says that matter is "physical substance in general, as distinct from mind and spirit; (in physics) that which occupies space and possesses mass, especially as distinct from energy."

Here's the scientific complication to these *substantial* things you *think* you see: *all matter is 99.999999999% space.* Every atom in existence with its miniscule electron "planets" flying round its miniscule proton-neutron "sun" is pretty much like our solar system. Calculate the amount of matter compared with space in every atom, and you get the 99.999999999% space that exists in nature, in your body, in the entire world, in the universe, and in the chair you are sitting on. You can see the chair, it feels solid, it's supporting you, but... it's mostly only space, or ether, or energy, depending on who's talking. Magnetic, quantum, or attractive forces like gravity make things seem hard, but... your chair is mainly—times a few million—nothing.

You see, touch, and taste matter. You smell particles in the air. You hear sound waves made by things. But there's more to what meets the five senses than this three-dimensional world.

Beyond, yet still an integral part of this world, is the fourth-dimensional Astral Plane—the realm of your dream life, imagination, and soul. Composed of vibrations which create energy, it's not something "out there," or "mystical," or even "new age." The Astral Plane has always been, and continues to be, here and now. It's your connection to your "higher self," to God the Creator. The Astral Plane is your birthright, though you might have to refresh your memory!

Swami Muktananda showed me how thin the veil is between our third and fourth-dimensional selves and how to access all-that-is by simply "seeing." He used *Chaktipat* to open my third eye.

You can learn how to experience this phenomenon. Everyone has the tools required—intention, passion, and trust—but these must be nurtured and developed.

Intention is the first step in imagining then focusing

on your goal. Hong set his heart and mind on drawing and painting. I clearly sought out insight and understanding from the guru.

Passion provides the energy to create and complete the tasks. Hong loved to draw cats and that kept him on his trek through the countryside as he wore out his sandals. I loved the guru and the opportunity to learn from him.

Trust in the divine gives you faith in yourself and your destination. Hong trusted his artistic abilities and his belief that the Creator of All Things had put him on the earth to draw. I trusted the message and gift from Muktananda, but also trusted my own voice which guided me to continue on my path and not join his journey.

Imagination, more than practical reality, kept me sane as a young boy. I believed my mother when she explained that if I worked hard enough, I could do or be anything. I told her I wanted to travel the world, write stories, and act in plays. Her response was always the same, "Yes, follow your dreams. You can do whatever you want."

My dad, the harsh voice of practicality, worked to keep me grounded. "Stop daydreaming. Pay attention. No excuses." I heard those words often.

Caught between my parent's two beliefs, I often felt that I didn't fit into the established order of society. My youthful frustration resulted in a medically diagnosed ulcer at age ten, but my youthful imagination had compelled me to write a story at age eight. "The Mystery Artist" was about a boy-mouse named Ricky who loved to draw, color and paint.

*Ricky drew pictures of fantasy and reality rearranged. One of purple tennis shoes with wings, flying amidst clouds of orange and green. Another about a red kangaroo on a pogo stick, hopping upside down. A third of a clock with time running all over the place.*

*When he shared his creations at school to his friends and teachers, the response was intimidating.*

*"Yuck!"*

*"That's not right."*

*"Your pictures are weird, Ricky, just like you…"*

*Beaten down by the comments from his friends and teachers, Ricky hid his artwork under his bed, but continued painting in private and hatched a bold plan. Early one morning as the mouse community slept, he tied a red wagon to the back of his bicycle and pedaled to the town's museum with his treasure trove of artwork. The museum was closed, so he slipped ten unsigned pictures under the front doors, returned home, and crawled back into bed.*

*Upon opening the museum, the curator marveled at the works and showed them to the staff. "How creative! Unlike anything, we've ever seen. Innocent yet provocative…"*

*"But they're not signed!" exclaimed a staff member. "Who's the artist?"*

*The search began. The local newspaper ran a spread featuring three of Ricky's masterpieces under the headline, "Who is the Mystery Artist?"*

*Ricky came forward proudly. The museum displayed all ten of his works, and in a ceremony in front of the entire school, Ricky signed each one.*

*From that day forth, Ricky was recognized as a fine artist, indeed.*

I wrote that story about Rickey in one afternoon and spent the next two days drawing crude pictures from my imagination. I fashioned it into a picture book and carried it to school.

Mrs. Hanson, my second-grade teacher, looked it over, and then peered down at me over the cover. "Where did you hear or read this story?"

"I made it up," I said.

"I don't think so, Jerry." She shook her head and squinted her eyes. "Where'd you find it? Tell me the truth."

"I'm telling the truth, Mrs. Hanson. It's mine."

She scrutinized me for a long uncomfortable moment, and then said, "Very well. It's a good story, but your spelling and handwriting are terrible. And the pictures need a lot of work. Here's what we'll do. Write more stories and bring them to me. I'll help with your writing. Maybe some of your friends can help you draw better."

Forty-five years later, *The Mystery Artist* was published in 1996 and sold 200,000 copies in school book fairs throughout the United States. I'll always appreciate Mrs. Hanson!

Perhaps like me, you felt estranged during your childhood. Were you the odd one out, the problem child, the dreamer, the one who just didn't seem to fit in? Though born with an innate connection to the fourth-dimensional Astral Plane, many people struggle to find a balance between grounded reality and their higher selves. It's an integral aspect of the journey.

Nature can be the magnificent teacher who validates your intention, stirs your passion, and strengthens your trust. And invites you to experience the truth and beauty that's right in front of you. Mother Earth provides more than a sustainable planet, but also the essence of the divine, visible to anyone willing to *see*.

My neighborhood friend Duane and I shared many choice adventures during our teenage years. This one is as clear in my mind as the glistening sea filling my vision right now.

One summer we were driving from Glenwood Springs, Colorado back home to Denver. Five miles into the ride as we curled through the mountain valley, Duane said, "Let's hike up to Hanging Lake."

"Okay!" I'd never been there, but I was game.

Soon we pulled off the road. Wearing tennis shoes, t-shirts, and jeans, we set off into the woods. Duane knew the way and took the lead. Young, fit and care-free, we climbed the steep trail in half an hour. Dog tired and drenched in sweat, we arrived at a natural geologic wonder, a small pristine lake suspended on a rock-cliff with a series of crystal-clear waterfalls spilling into it. A forest of tall pine trees stood like Mother Nature's sentinels protecting three sides of the lake.

The water in Hanging Lake, blue, green, turquoise and clear, mesmerized me. I could see to the bottom. "How deep?"

"Over your head," and with a mischievous grin, Duane added, "Let's go for a swim."

I hesitated. "It looks cold."

"Come on. No one else is here. Cowboy up."

"Are you serious?"

Duane put his hand on my shoulder and pointed toward the middle of the lake. "See the log halfway across? We can walk out to the center, and then it'll only be a short swim to the other side."

I nodded yes, and we were naked within a minute.

We ran to the submerged log resting on the shore-line and began to traverse the slippery bark to the center of the small lake.

"I'll go first," Duane said. He dove in, surfaced with a scream, swam hard, and crossed the water in no time. He climbed out, holding his sides. "Do it, Jerry. You've got to do it!"

I dove in and immediately thought I was about to die. The icy water pierced and numbed my body in an instant. Arms stroking and legs pumping, I howled "Eeeaawwghhh!" so loud that a flock of chickadees flew from the trees. Somehow, I made it to shore. Duane grabbed my outstretched arms and helped me stand. I jumped up and down with frigid water cascading from my body. Still holding on, Duane jumped along with me in our naked dance. We then ran along the shoreline, hopped over moss-covered rocks, and circled through the pine trees, laughing long and loud, again and again.

With all my senses, raw and tingling, I'd never felt so happy to be alive. As we hiked back down to the car, I said, "Thanks, buddy. It was amazing."

"Yup. I knew you'd like it."

That day, Nature showed us how full of life we were, bursting with energy and joy.

Your dreams become real when you embrace pure intention, passion, and trust. Mother Earth gives you the stage to play out your dreams. Nature everywhere presents myriad ways for you to *see*. Beyond your five senses, you expand your mind to understand, engage your heart to feel, and trust that your belief in God the Creator is genuine. Everything becomes possible. Cats leap off the canvas, a swami opens third eyes, and an artist named Ricky is encouraged and rewarded.

~ ~ ~

# Work

---

## CHAPTER FIVE

*At the moment
of commitment,
the universe conspires
to assist you.*

~Goethe~

# The Laughing Brothers

## China

A LONG TIME AGO, THREE YOUNG CHINESE MONKS began traveling together. Fu, Pen, and Niu were not brothers by birth—they chose to be brothers, united in a mission to help heal humanity through laughter. As the years of their journeys wore on, they became known as "The Laughing Brothers."

Upon arriving in small villages or larger towns, the three monks went to marketplaces, stood in a triangle to create an energy field of felicity, and simply laughed. And laughed. And laughed.

Fu always started with a shout to his younger brothers, "Who's getting fat today?"

"You are!" yelled Pen and Niu in unison.

"Indeed, I am!"

Fu was extremely thin, and they found this extremely funny. A chuckle from Pen and a snicker from Niu sent Fu into hysterics. When the townsfolk heard this resounding chorus of hilarity coming from the undulating bodies of three strange monks, they initially stopped and stared. Eventually someone in the crowded marketplace just had to laugh. The monks' merriment was infectious and spread throughout the crowd. Soon everyone, young or old, was laughing loud and long, and for a moment, a new and better world opened.

The Laughing Brothers wandered throughout China for decades, bringing cheer to all, and charming people wherever they went. As folks laughed along with the monks, they felt the possibility of transformation deep within.

One day in a remote village, Fu clutched his chest at the height of a huge guffaw and fell face first to the ground. He lay still… and silent… and would laugh no more. For a few moments, Pen and Niu stood like statues gazing down at their departed brother.

The villagers inched closer. An elderly man approached the brothers and said, "I'm so sorry for your loss. You must be very sad."

The two monks lifted their heads and looked into each other's eyes. Their lips pursed into a smirk, which quickly shifted into a childlike grin. They grabbed each other's arms and danced in a circle around Fu. Shouting for joy and laughing wildly, they pranced down the street in celebration of their brother's death!

The villagers were shocked. Some grew angry and followed them, yelling, "Stop it! This is disgraceful! Show some respect for the dead!"

Pen whirled around and faced the crowd with a serious smile on his face. "You dear people don't understand… yet. Years ago, we bet on who would die first. Fu bet on himself, and today he won! He defeated Niu and me! The three of us traveled and laughed together for a lifetime. How could we send our brother into the beyond with anything but laughter?"

Niu peeked his head over Pen's shoulder. "It's the only possible farewell for a man who has spent his entire life laughing. If we don't celebrate, Fu will think we are fools who have fallen back into the trap."

Pen's raised eyebrows wrinkled the skin all the way up to his bald head. "How can laughter die?"

"It can't," Niu answered.

"How can a spirit that is truly alive ever die?" With each word, Pen pointed to individual people in the crowd. "The spirit in you… and you… and you… the spirit in all of us?"

"It can't die." Niu shook his head back and forth as he spoke slowly. "Not… even… if… you… want… it… to."

The villagers calmed down and went about their business. When time came for the cremation, a group of them offered to help. "We'll bathe and dress Fu for you," the village headman said, "as ritual prescribes."

"Thank you, but please… no," said Pen. "Fu didn't like rituals and wanted nothing of the sort. He insisted that we do not bathe him, that we do not change his clothing. I remember his exact words: 'Place me on the burning pyre as I am.' We must follow his wishes."

Later that night under a bright full moon, the villagers gently placed Fu on top of the pyre and then formed a circle around it. The village headman lit the fire below with a torch. When the flames traveled upward through the pile of sticks and logs and finally licked the body, something amazing unfolded. A whoosh! A pop! A deafening bang! Everyone was startled, including Nui and Pen.

Bright flashes of red, blue, green, and yellow burst in the sky, cavorting with the moon and illuminating the dark clouds. The ahh-struck villagers were entranced with the dazzling display that concluded with a big boisterous ka-boom!

To play the final joke, Fu had hidden fireworks throughout his clothing! His long life proved that he who laughs, lasts. And he got the last laughs, too! Pen and Niu laughed uproariously, the people laughed with them, and soon their tears of laughter evolved into tears of pure joy.

Fu's body turned to ash, but neither his laughter nor his spirit died. As Fu passed on, he passed on the laughter and gave everyone a fresh breath of life.

~ ~ ~

# Pleasant Journeys

## Boulder, Colorado, 1970

A FIERCE MIDNIGHT RAIN PELTED the front window of my cabin as I sat at my desk with a storm in my soul. I hadn't slept for three days and nights which had merged into an unfathomable abyss. A major research paper was due in two days, and no matter how hard I slaved, I ran into dead ends. My fellowship from the University of Colorado in Boulder depended on maintaining a B average. Without it, I'd lose my sole means of educational support for my Ph.D. in Rhetoric, Public Address, and Literature.

I pulled out the bottom drawer to get a file, saw my 22-caliber pistol, and envisioned a one-way street out. I picked up the gun and felt its weight in my hand. *Hefty. Capable. Effective.* I plodded over to the closet and returned to my desk with a box of ammunition. Holding the pistol in my right hand, I slowly inserted the bullets with my left, and then pressed the gun barrel to my right temple. I'd arrived at a to-be-or-not-to-be crisis in my life at age 27.

"Death would be so much easier," I sobbed.

The crisis had many facets, and one was named Brenda. A shapely, 25-year-old English major, she was intelligent, well-spoken, and had a great sense of humor. Her auburn hair, brown eyes, and kissable lips had initially attracted me, and we'd been dating for five months.

At the end of an evening together, Brenda had asked, "When are we going to have sex?"

"I… I don't know."

"Well, I'm ready," she purred.

I paused and concocted an excuse. "I'm sorry, but I gotta finish some homework. Let's get you back to your dorm."

That night on her doorstep was the last time I ever kissed Brenda.

The day after I'd brought her to a family Christmas dinner, my mother called to launch the big question. "When will you announce your engagement?"

"Let's wait and see, Mom. I'm in no hurry."

"You've waited a *long time* to find her. Have you two talked about marriage?"

"Not yet."

"I think she's right for you. Don't let her get away."

1970 was a turbulent year for me, and for the United States. Racism flourished in spite of the historic Civil Rights Act in the '60s. The Vietnam War butchered our soldiers abroad and tore apart our country at home. The Ohio National Guard killed four protesting students at Kent State University. "Tricky Dick" Nixon was President, and the Watergate scandal dominated the news headlines.

One of the greatest films of all time, *2001: A Space Odyssey*, had arrived two years earlier and introduced the world to HAL, the Heuristically programmed Algorithmic computer that controlled the spacecraft.

"Open the pod bay doors, HAL."

I'd used that line to terminate conversations with friends and colleagues. It was funny until the night I held a gun to my head. The pistol was like HAL: cold, metal, and in control. Heuristic comes from a Greek word meaning "I find, I discover." Heuristic programs are designed to solve problems more quickly when classic methods are too slow. They trade optimum solutions, completeness, or precision for speed. A short cut. But that night HAL wouldn't cooperate, and I felt helpless, lost in space and time.

It hurts down deep to live a lie, deeper than a pill could ever reach. Brenda, the fellowship, the writer's block, the exhaustion and stress were merely catalysts, and the simple core of my point-blank crisis rose up through my being—no rhetoric required, just the truth. Regurgitating bile, I said aloud, "I'm a faggot."

Fate pulled the trigger before I could, and three words shot into my mind.

"I need help."

I'd never really asked for help. That thought weakened my resolve. A few moments later, my hand laid the pistol on the desk, and my body collapsed onto the bed—dead tired but alive.

I awoke the next morning, ready to seek help. The slim Boulder phone book contained only three listings for psychiatrists. Due to its ordinariness, one name stood out—Dr. Robert Johnson. At 9:00 a.m. I dialed the number and was surprised to hear the man answer.

After a five-minute conversation, he said, "Unload the pistol. Dig a hole in your yard and bury the bullets, all of them. Meet me in my office in one hour."

Dr. Johnson was tall, thin, and had a firm handshake. His eyes were kind and his voice resonant. He'd recently moved to Boulder with his family and was still organizing his office. A half-empty bookcase lined one wall. Fat file-folders covered the top of his expansive wooden desk. A painting of a Colorado mountain at sunset provided the only color in the room.

He motioned to a tufted leather sofa. "Sit, Jerry. Let's talk." He rolled over his desk chair and faced me. "You look nervous."

"My world is falling apart. And I don't have much money. And I don't know if I can afford you."

"We'll work something out. Tell me what's happening, and I mean *everything*."

With shoulders slumped and my head bowed, I unburdened my soul, including Keir Dullea's command to HAL from *The Space Odyssey*. "Open the pod bay doors, HAL." I opened up my inner doors for this man. I told him about Brenda and the pressure from my mother. I told him about how I'd always felt different but never knew exactly why. I told him about being at a drive-in at age seventeen with my two best friends and watching a movie that suggested a hint of male-to-male love. As the final credits rolled, one friend had asked, "What would you do if you were queer?" I shuddered and said, "Kill myself."

Dr. Johnson asked a few questions, listened carefully, and at the end of the 45-minute "hour," stunned me with his astute summation.

"First, there's nothing wrong with you. Homosexuality isn't unnatural. Medical opinions are shifting, and I'm in the camp that says you don't need to change to be happy. And I doubt you can change, anyway." He smiled warmly. "Second, you're an intelligent young man with a full life ahead. You've accomplished a lot and have more to contribute. And yes, you can find happiness, even love."

I could feel the weight of my world lifting from my shoulders, but one question still held them down. He answered it without my asking.

"Third, if you can afford $100 total, your fee will be ten bucks for today and then fifteen for the next sessions. I'd like to meet with you six more times during the next two months."

Tears blurred my eyes, and he handed me a tissue. I agreed to the terms and follow-up appointments.

We met on Thursday mornings focusing on two agendas—dealing with my coming out in the repressed social climate of 1968, and my desires for a creative future.

"Do you want to leave the academic world behind?"

"I'm seventy-percent certain," I said. "After teaching at the University of Massachusetts and here in Boulder, I'm not thrilled by the prospect of an academic career. I want more creativity, more action."

In our final session, I told him of my decision to leave school and travel throughout Mexico. I was ready to begin my search for a satisfying future.

"You must visit Zihuantanejo," said the good doctor, "a small fishing village on Mexico's Pacific Coast, about 150 miles northwest of Acapulco. I've been there twice with my family. There's something special about it."

"I'll find it."

Shaking my hand for the last time, he added, "I'm here if you ever need me."

"Thank you… thank you for everything."

After borrowing a few hundred dollars from my older brother, I purchased a portable typewriter and stuffed my backpack for a journey into the unknown. I flew from Denver to Tucson, Arizona and boarded a bus to cross the border into Nogales, Mexico.

An elderly gentleman passenger in the seat across from me asked, "What's in the case?"

"A portable typewriter."

"Can I have a look?"

I opened the case and handed it over.

"It's beautiful. I've never before seen one this small. What are you, a reporter?"

"No, sir. I write poetry and short stories."

"You any good?"

I tilted my head and raised an eyebrow. "I'm working at it."

"Where are you getting off the bus?"

"Mazatlán. I want to spend a week there."

"Ahh," he sighed. "The Pearl of the Pacific! A great place. Where will you stay?"

"I don't know yet. You have any suggestions?"

"Check out Maggie's Guest House. It's three or four blocks back from the beach. Three stories tall and covered in large flat stones painted in bright colors. You can't miss it. And Maggie is a gem. Speaks English like a native and treats her guests like family. Wait'll you taste her chicken soup!"

Maggie lived up to the man's testimonial. She rented me a large room on the top floor with a view of the cathedral and the *Zócalo*, or town square. "Señor Jerry, you can't experience Mazatlán in just one week," explained Maggie. "I'm putting you down for two."

I stayed in Mazatlán four weeks and relished every

Sunday lunch at Maggie's—incredible chicken soup with cumin, crushed tortilla chips, and sour cream. Each day offered adventure, whether walking barefoot on the beach, enjoying the afternoon sun in the Zócalo, or meeting friendly locals and other travelers. I awoke with a smile each morning.

One day I sat in the park reading *Justine*, the first novel of *The Alexandria Quartet* by Lawrence Durrell. Engrossed in the fiction, I paid little attention to a Mexican boy, who had appeared in front of me.

"Señor, señor! Can I speak English with you?"

I set the paperback on my lap and looked up. "Sure. What's your name?"

"Domingo," he said and joined me on the bench.

"Good name. I'm Jerry." Rather formally, he shook my hand. I guessed he was about 15.

"Were you born here in Mazatlán, Domingo?"

"Si, I mean… yes."

After ten minutes of hit-or-miss conversation, he pointed to my tennis shoes. "How big feet?"

"You mean… what size are they?"

"Si, yes."

"Ten."

Kicking off his timeworn, dusty sandals, Domingo exclaimed, "Size ten! I try?"

Not wanting to disappoint the boy, I untied my shoes and handed them over. With a grin, he slipped on my shoes, said "Gracias," then turned and ran away faster than I believed possible.

Dumbfounded, I arrived back at Maggie's wearing Domingo's tired sandals.

"Got you in the park, eh?" asked Sandra, a heavily tattooed, Canadian hippy. "It's an old trick. Now you've contributed to the community. Growing boys need new shoes."

I loved wandering through the Zócalo on Saturday nights. A small carnival created a festive atmosphere with live music, dancing, food carts, and games. Young people cruised the perimeter, boys walking one direction to see the girls walking in the opposite direction, an age-old ritual in Mexico. I always paused to watch the classic baseball toss games. When a boy threw the ball at the milk bottles and missed, even at 9 p.m., his friends had a ready excuse. "The sun was in his eyes."

Falling in love with the Mexican people, culture, music, and cuisine, was easy. Trying to capture all the activity and emotions by pecking at my typewriter for two hours each day took a lot of work.

Chris and Ron arrived during my fourth week in Mazatlán, the third time they'd driven their yellow-and-white Volkswagen bus from San Francisco to Mexico. They were committed partners, genuinely friendly, queer and unashamed of it. After lunch and too many beers, I became their pet project.

"So, you're a homo, right?" asked Chris, his voice deep. Caucasian, tall, handsome and toned, he was easy on the eyes.

"I guess so."

"No bullshit now!"

"Okay. Yes, I'm queer." It felt amazing to say it aloud.

"How much experience have you had with guys?"

"Not much. I've made out, and a bit more…"

"Still a virgin!" sang out Ron, his voice melodious. Born "Renaldo" in Buenos Aries, Ron's golden-brown Brazilian skin seemed to glow, and not just due to the beer. He was 23, five years younger and a few inches shorter than his partner. Ron spoke fluent Spanish and often took the lead in conversations. "We have much to teach you. We're going to drag you out of the closet, toot sweet!"

"Toot sweet?" I asked. "How fast is that?"

"Up to you. If you swished like me, you'd be out in a flash. But you don't look or act queer, so you come out whenever you want."

"We're driving to Mexico City on Saturday morning," Chris announced, "and you're coming with us. You can help pay for the gas."

"And just so you know," Ron said, "even though you're kinda cute, we won't be sleeping with you."

"We're committed to each other," Chris added.

I felt somewhat relieved. "I'm okay with that!"

"It's a big faggot world out there," Ron said, gesturing to everywhere else. "So, what's your type, honey?"

"My type?"

"Who do you want to bed?"

"Hmm… someone my age, or younger… fit, an athletic body? I like swimmers."

"Who doesn't?" asked Chris. "We'll show you all kinds of guys in the city. You like brown skin, right?"

"I do."

The trip to Mexico City took two days. Once ensconced in an inexpensive, clean hotel in the center of town, they took me to a "mixed cantina" frequented by straight and gay men.

"Be careful when you use the pisser," Chris warned with a smile. "Lots of guys are looking you over."

Traditional Mexican ballads, or *corridos*, pounded out of the speakers in the crowded bar. Songs of lost love, criminals escaping justice, and heroes dying bounced off the walls. Many patrons with arms around each other sung along to an audience of Corona beer bottles packed on the table tops in front of them.

I leaned in close to Ron. "What should I do if someone tries to grope me?"

"Say no *intervenecionsta!* Like it you mean it and they'll understand."

I said it and meant it three times that night, twice in the toilet and once at the table. I had to admit, however, that I liked it, at least a bit.

"Tomorrow we're taking you to one of the biggest saunas in Mexico City," Chris said as we left the cantina. "It's hot, fun and a great way to relax."

"Sounds good to me." I had no clue what a complete surprise and awakening this would be.

"It's not especially queer," Ron said. "Guys like guys differently in Mexico than in the US. Most are straight, but still, enjoy the companionship of other guys."

"Especially when they're naked and sweating together," Chris added.

We arrived around noon. The two-story sauna, filled with teenaged, middle-aged, and elderly men wearing white towels and nothing else, proved to be a shock. Rows of lockers, open shower rooms, and massage beds filled every niche. The place smelled of eucalyptus, sweat, and maleness. Many older guys had their arms around the shoulders of younger men. Smiles abounded.

The three of us sweated in the blazing hot sauna for ten minutes and then cooled down under cold showers. While drying off, Ron asked me, "Ever had a massage?"

"No, should I?"

"Definitely! I'll fix you up." He pointed to a dark, muscled man wearing red gym shorts. "That's Mario. He's good, seriously good." After speaking to the masseur, Ron motioned me over to the slim clean-sheeted bed. "Lay on your front, close your eyes, and relax. He'll take care of you."

Mario stripped my towel away the moment I lay down. With his strong experienced hands, he began at my neck and shoulders, rubbing downward inch by inch to my bare ass, and on to my legs. Pleasure flooded through my body. His touch, professional and intimate, gave me an erection. Thank God, I was on my belly!

Anticipating the finale for a newbie, several men gathered to watch as my encounter progressed. Mario spent the final five minutes of the thirty-minute massage attending to my butt. Firm fingers caressed my glutes while long thumbs explored my inner nerve endings. I'd never felt anything like it and suspected that my body contained mysteries yet undiscovered. I muffled a moan. The watchers laughed, and Mario tossed me a clean towel.

"God," I said aloud in the shower with cool water pounding on my back. "What the hell?"

Chris shouted from outside the shower room, "You okay, Jerry?"

"Yeah, I think so."

"Laugh it off. We'll have more fun tonight."

We did indeed have fun that night and non-stop fun continued for the next three weeks. I loved traveling with my first gay friends, contributing to the cost of fuel, having adventures, and entertaining possibilities for my future.

We stopped in Guanajuato, high in the mountains of central Mexico and renowned for its silver mining history and colonial architecture. Overwhelmed by its beauty, I felt like a child discovering a new world— exotic vibrant colors on houses clinging to steep hills, churches imbued with grace, shady plazas offering rest, and college students wanting to practice their English. Though I was prepared for the scam, none of them asked to try on my shoes.

After two weeks, Chris and Ron said they were moving on, but I decided to stay for another week.

"What will you take away from Guanajuato, Jerry?" Chris asked as they were ready to head out.

"Silver bells calling me to services every morning."

"You don't go to church," Ron teased.

"The bells resonate with me, not the religion. Besides, I have nothing to confess."

"Nothing to confess! That's a great motto. Don't forget it."

"I'll try, but I will never forget all the moments we shared together. Thank you so much for everything." I hugged my friends and watched them drive away in the dusty van.


Traveling solo, I found sweet refuge in San Blas, Nayarit, a fishing village on the Pacific Coast. Built on a swamp and surrounded by jungle, San Blas hosted a few people and a bevy of herons, turtles and exotic birds.

I found an affable boatman named Mateo who spoke English and paid him a few pesos to ferry me across the waterway separating the town from a gorgeous coral beach. With Mateo's sinewy arms pulling and pushing the oars, our banter became a ritual on the crossing. He'd point out motionless crocodiles near the shore and say, chuckling, "Don't jump in, Señor Jerry!"

"Any jaguars around here?"

"No, big boa constrictors!" Late one afternoon I climbed from the beach into the boat and sat beside an ancient man dressed in his indigenous attire. Three differently sized, brightly colored bags, or bolsas, hung from his neck.

Mateo noticed me staring at the mystical symbols intricately woven into the cotton and wool fabric. "You like, Señor Jerry? He's one of the Huichol people. Their men weave power into their bolsas."

"They're amazing. What's the small one for?"

"Peyote."

Recognizing my interest in his bolsa, the old man handed it to me for a closer look. I held up the narrow magenta and azure blue strap attached to the bolsa and underneath the pouch bounced six woolen balls, two per string. I felt a warmth emanating from the bolsa, and my eyes grew wide with curiosity.

Mateo talked with the Huichol man in Spanish and then turned to me. "Señor Jerry. He said he will sell it for twenty U.S. dollars."

I hesitated. Twenty dollars was a serious strain on my budget. I started to hand it back and discovered I didn't want to let it go.

"Okay. We'll walk to my casa. I'll pay in dollars." Not until six weeks later did I grasp how the magical bolsa would play a vital role in my life's work.

After three days in Acapulco, I boarded a rickety rusted bus to travel the 150 miles to the sleepy fishing village of Zihuatanejo. The roads matched the bus for wear. Eight bone-jarring hours later, I arrived in paradise.

An energetic, clever, 16-year-old kid greeted me at the bus station, grabbed my pack, and hoisted it onto his back. "My name is Jorge! Nice to meet you. I speak English, Señor, and I know the best places to stay."

Charmed by the lad's boldness, I followed him up a narrow trail that wound up and over a lush green hill. Overlooking turquoise waters in the cove below stood a one-room casita topped with a red tin roof. An empty hammock hanging between the veranda's wooden posts beckoned to me.

"It's perfect," I sighed. "Can I afford it?"

"Si, Señor. My mother owns it. She likes gringos. They pay in advance."

I paid in advance. Soon I fell into a daily rhythm, eating fresh-caught seafood in small cafes, sliding down the steep embankment from my abode each afternoon, riding the gentle waves, and sleeping soundly each night, alone in my bed.

My three-dimensional, technicolor dreams were full of action and drama. An entire week of dreams placed me in huge gift-wrapped boxes. Pinholes of light poured in from the lids, and music drifted in from above. In each dream, I needed to find an escape route. Tipping the box over proved successful, and as I emerged into the light, an audience cheered. I awoke every morning with a smile in my heart.

Interacting with the locals, tourists, and genuine hippies came naturally. We celebrated friendship with tequila and beer, but when offered tokes of skunky smelling weed, I declined. The Mexican Federal Police, as well as the local cops, frightened me.

After my first week, I asked Jorge to take my dirty clothes to the local laundry.

"I will bring them back in two days. They must dry in the sun." He didn't share the fact that he planned to wear my Levi jeans and shirt to the local dance that night. Nor did he plan on me showing up at the dance.

The moment I laid eyes on Jorge, showing off his attire to his friends, he blushed red and shouted, "Hola, Señor Jerry!"

"Hola, Jorge," I hollered back. "I like your new clothes!"

"Gracias, Señor. It is just for tonight I wear them."

"I know, Jorge." He returned my laundry, pressed

and clean, two days later.

Pages in my journal filled and overflowed as I recorded my feelings, experiences, hopes, and dreams. At the end of each day's jottings, I wrote down a statement

*I'll live openly as a gay man, no matter what.*

*I'll learn how to meditate. I must find a way inside.*

*I'll make a living telling stories.*

*The Huichol bolsa will be my story bag and hold hundreds of stories. I'll wear it with pride.*

After five months I was no longer the same man, and it was time to return home. Needing a bit more funds for plane fare, I sold the portable typewriter to my landlady, Jorge's mother. I gave Jorge my clean Levi's. He was thrilled.

After the excruciating, multi-hour bus ride to Acapulco, I flew to Denver. The next day I met with the chairman of the University of Colorado Communications Department in Boulder.

"Your timing is good," Professor Martin Cobin said. "Yesterday I received a letter from the University of Washington in Seattle. One of their professors has fallen seriously ill, and they want you to teach his classes beginning in three weeks."

"That's great. But what about my dissertation?"

"Write it there for now, then come back next summer and finish it."

I arrived in Seattle mid-September of 1970, and found a city filled with possibilities and pulsating with creative energy. Music, dance, theater, art, cuisine, and coffee flourished. The Age of Aquarius had come to pass. Living openly as a gay man, I made friends, enjoyed sex, and experienced each day as another adventure. I taught speech and literature for two years at the university before chucking my academic career.

"I'm going to make a living telling stories," I told my colleagues.

"How will you pay the rent?" one asked.

"I'll find a way."

Seattle's larger churches had created pop-up coffee houses in their basements on Saturday nights and offered their stages to performers. Interweaving multicultural folk and fairy tales, myths, legends, and a few true stories, I began sharing with a variety of audiences: adult, family, kids—whoever ventured into the room. My battered fedora, upturned on a table near the door, accepted the coins and bills given by my listeners. To make ends meet, I worked as a house painter, short-order cook, and a junior high teacher in the Seattle Public Schools.

One Saturday night after telling tales in the basement of St. Joseph's Catholic Church on Seattle's Capitol Hill, I counted the money in the hat. $28.67. My one-bedroom apartment cost $85 a month. One hour of work provided one-third of my rent! I proclaimed myself a Professional Storyteller, and never looked back.

In 1971, five of my male ancestors paid me a visit in a dream. I said hello to an aged, gnarled, and bearded man, an American pioneer that I recognized from old family photos—my great-great-grandfather, Pleasant DeSpain Sr. Behind him stood his oldest son, Pleasant Jr. I nodded, and Junior nodded back. Beside him was Alan Pleasant, my long-deceased grandfather. And in his arms rested Pleasant Sonny, the boy who would have been my uncle, had he not died so young.

A wave of connection and love filled the dream. I awoke knowing the time had come to change my name. I consulted with trusted friends who agreed that "Pleasant DeSpain" offered a name as unique as my newborn profession. Three months later, with acceptance from the Seattle courts, I became the fifth-generation Pleasant in the DeSpain family.

I printed posters announcing storytelling programs in intimate theaters, coffee houses, and on the street. My friends helped to plaster them on telephone poles, fences, and storefront windows around Seattle. My theme-based shows included "Tales of Love and Loss," "Trickster Tales," and "Heroes: Yesterday and Today."

Rehearsing for hours each day and learning what listeners enjoyed hearing, I developed my stage persona, while refining my storytelling chops and bringing in cash to keep me going. Seattle elementary school librarians called and asked me to share stories with a class or two. I asked for a nominal fee of $25 plus lunch. Then came invitations to spend entire school days with hundreds of students seated on gym floors. I upped my fee to $100 which included four, 45-minute programs, two in the morning and two in the afternoon. Returning home after each school day, exhausted but pleased, I felt the flush of success.

My reputation grew, and in the summer of 1975, the mayor officially proclaimed me, "Seattle's Resident Storyteller." That was a proud day for me, but also made me consider other possibilities with a larger audience, I decided to create a children's television show.

"I want to enliven imaginations in living rooms of homes," I told TR, one of my best friends, "A show with no Show and Tell, only tell. I'll just tell my stories and let them imagine the rest."

"What does that look like?" he asked.

"Well… definitely no puppets, costumes, drawings or props like all the other shows."

"How about music?"

"Maybe theme music to open and close the show. That's it."

Early one morning as I drove across the floating bridge spanning Lake Washington, majestic Mount Rainier broke from her usual cloud cover to bask in the golden light. Marveling at the sight, I inhaled and knew what I'd call my show. *Pleasant Journeys.*

The four television studios serving the greater Seattle area were national network affiliates for ABC, NBC, CBS, and Public Broadcasting. I made separate appointments with their four program directors and soon became discouraged. Public Broadcasting had no funding, and two of the directors rejected my concept of pure storytelling on television.

My last hope was with the largest station covering Seattle and beyond, the NBC affiliate, King-TV. The appointment to meet with Program Director Bob Guy was set for 9 a.m. on Thursday. On Wednesday, his assistant called. "Mr. Guy is unavailable tomorrow. Can you come in next week?"

She rescheduled the meeting for the following Thursday. I got a déjà vu phone call the next Wednesday. "Sorry. Mr. Guy will be out of town tomorrow. Can we set you up for next week?"

"Would next Thursday at 9 a.m. work for him?" I asked as politely as I could muster.

"Yes. See you then."

Frustrated, but still hopeful, I visited the University Book Store to purchase a recent collection of traditional British folktales. I handed it to the cashier, a middle-aged woman with reading glasses pinched onto the end of her nose. She examined the book, front and back. "This looks interesting."

I reached for my wallet. "I've read good reviews."

Abruptly, in a lower voice, she said, "King-TV."

I squinted and shook my head. "What did you say?"

She blinked and returned to her normal voice. "Your book looks interesting."

For one moment in time, the entire universe seemed to channel a message to me through that one person in front of me. That moment hardened my resolve to connect with King-TV. I wasn't going to be turned away again from my meeting with Mr. Guy. I unplugged my phone answering machine and refused to answer any incoming calls for the next three days. I arrived at the King-TV station on time for my 9 a.m. appointment and finally met his exasperated assistant.

"I've tried to reach you several times," she said. "He can't see you today."

The door to the director's office opened. Mr. Bob Guy, disheveled, unshaven, a cigarette dangling from his hand, glanced at me and growled, "What'd'ya want?"

"To create a storytelling program for kids."

He frowned and stubbed out his cigarette in the ashtray on the assistant's desk. "I'll give you ten minutes. Come in."

The office reflected the disorder in the man's life. The overloaded desk spilled folders and papers onto the floor. A dirty sweater covered the back of the guest chair. Bad lighting and stale smoke consumed the room.

The king of King-TV settled into his throne behind the desk. "Talk," he grunted. "And don't waste my time."

I sat on the guest chair with the sweater, took a deep breath, and launched into my proposal. "A weekly Sunday morning show called *Pleasant Journeys*. I'll tell three or four, theme-based tales. I don't need props or costumes. I'd like a wooden stool in front of a large tree, with a blue sky and white clouds in the background. It'll be affordable, creative, and I'll inspire imaginations on the other side of the screen."

Mr. Bob Guy put his hand up like a traffic cop. "Stop there. Tell me a story but keep it short."

I shared an old English nursery rhyme—"This Is the House That Jack Built"—with my audience of one. In three minutes, surly Mr. Guy transformed into a simple guy, a kid on a journey through his imagination.

He wiped his wet eyes with his sleeve. "How did you know? That story was a favorite of mine as a boy. It takes me back to… oh, never mind…" After collecting himself, Bob gestured to his overflowing desk. "Somewhere in that mess is a contract… a contract I don't want to sign. We've shown *The Big Blue Marble* for the last two seasons, and they've doubled the price. I don't like the show, and I don't want it for a third season. The contract must be signed, or not, by the end of today."

He paused and stared at the mound on his desk, then cocked his head and looked me straight in the eye. "And here you are, Pleasant… with a possibility. I love storytelling. And I love the name *Pleasant Journeys*. I don't know if you have what it takes, but we can give it a try. I'll pay you $100 for the pilot. We'll tape it in two weeks. Now, get out of here."

Stunned and light-headed, I marveled at the timing of my proposal and the divine selection I'd made to tell the perfect story at that moment. Driving home, I yelled "Thank you, God!" again and again.

The pilot failed miserably due to over-telling my tales *without an audience*. I was accustomed to performing live, watching people's reactions, and feeling the energy in the room. Bob understood the problem. He saw the potential of the show and knew how to adjust the production. "We'll record it again next week with a dozen second and third graders in front of you."

That worked.

With an initial, thirteen-week contract prepared, Bob asked me to meet with him in his office. I sat down in front of his desk as he closed the door. He plopped into his chair and sighed. "Pleasant... we investigate on-air talent. You've come up clean in the report, but there's an issue we must discuss."

"Okay." I knew what was coming.

"Are you gay?"

"Yes."

"And you're out?"

"I am."

"I have no problem with your being gay, but you'll be representing this station with a children's show. It's a delicate situation."

"I won't do anything to jeopardize the show or the station."

"Any scandals and I'll cancel the show."

"I understand."

We signed the contract, and Bob reached over his desk to shake my hand. "I believe in you, Pleasant. I want this to work as much as you do."

The set he created for the show was marvelous— exactly as I'd imagined it. With kids sitting in front of me, I perched on a stool underneath a splendid, paper-mâché oak tree with knotholes and overhanging branches. The sky in the background changed to match the stories. I wore a simple vest, long-sleeved shirt, and khaki pants. The bolsa always hung from my neck, and I'd brush it with my fingers before telling a story.

After the show, kids would come up and ask, "What was in the bolsa?"

I'd bring out a crystal elephant and tell them, "The elephant has an amazing memory and helps me remember my stories." And a crystal turtle. "The turtle is a symbol of story in many cultures. In some it represents Mother Earth; in some Mother Earth is sitting on a turtle's back!"

The bolsa and turtle even inspired me to write a book—*Eleven Turtle Tales: Adventure Tales from Around the World*.

Pleasant on the set of *Pleasant Journeys*

*Pleasant Journeys* ran on King-TV every Sunday morning for five years. I wrote, produced, and hosted a total of 167 thirty-minute shows. Without the help of a teleprompter, I told more than 500 stories and activated the imaginations of children and adults at the studio and in their living rooms.

Along the way, and with Bob Guy's permission, I asked the entertainment editor of *The Seattle Times* if he'd consider adding a weekly column called *Pleasant Journeys*, so children could read a story published on Saturday and then hear me tell it on Sunday. The bonding of television and newspaper proved rewarding, and within a year, six other newspapers around the United States carried the column. My written tales were reaching a million readers a week.

During the second year of the show and column, a local book publisher asked me to compile stories for a book. It turned into a two-volume set with 44 tales, naturally entitled, *Pleasant Journeys*. I dedicated the first volume to a generous, creative, story-loving, and big-hearted man—Bob Guy. He cried when I presented him with the book.

Because of this fresh look at storytelling, local and national journalists requested interviews with me. I shared my experiences and talked about the importance of imaginations enlivened with stories told aloud. It wasn't long before I read of other tellers forging a similar path as mine. Several brave, talented, and committed souls were having success creating our contemporary profession.

In May of 1979, I received a call from a stranger. "I'm Jimmy Neil Smith in Jonesborough, Tennessee. How y'all doin'?"

"Just fine, thanks. How can I help you?"

"Well, I've been reading about you, Mr. Pleasant, and it's all good. We're having a weekend storytellin' festival in October. This'll be our seventh year. A lot of folks show up in our lil' Southern town to listen, and I'd like you to join us."

"It sounds great. Other storytellers will be there, too?"

"Yessir. Some o' your colleagues should be there,

along with some good friends y'all haven't met yet. Everyone has a grand time."

Jimmy Neil, a man my age, was on the same mission as me: to save and savor our oral traditions. Jonesborough, a historic destination in the heart of the Appalachian Mountains, was an ideal venue for sharing stories. Back in October 1973, Jimmy Neil invited local tellers to gather at an old farm wagon in the town's Courthouse Square for the first public event focused on and dedicated to the ancient tradition of storytelling. About 60 people turned out to listen.

That fall in 1979, hundreds arrived for a long weekend of listening. Jonesborough had no hotels, so local folks housed the tellers. We told stories on stage, inside giant circus tents, on lawns, and even in the local graveyard. After the scheduled programs, we pioneers of the profession gathered until the wee hours, telling tales from the long and winding road, our passion for the art, personal stories of how we believed in ourselves and knew that all things are possible.

Nowadays, ten-thousand people flock to Jonesborough every October to hear an extensive roster of amazing tellers, festivals abound in major cities, and storytelling programs are presented in schools and libraries throughout the world.

*Thank you, Jimmy Neil Smith, for your vision and the energy to make that dream become reality.*

My career has been a shared journey. Throughout the years of traveling, writing and telling, I've visited thousands of schools, libraries, churches, festivals, and theaters. More than 350 of my traditional, multicultural tales are in print. The work continues to satisfy me, but it's the people who offer me the gift of listening that I most appreciate.

*Thank you, Creator!*

My guardians, angels, meditation practice, belief in my mission, love of the art, even my luck, all came together for the creation of this "Pleasant Journeys" story. Had the universe led me to an old-school, clueless psychiatrist instead of progressive Dr. Robert Johnson who convinced me of my worthiness, I might have pulled the trigger in 1969. Dead men don't write.

~ ~ ~

# The Universe Conspires

CONSCIOUSNESS, BOTH HUMAN AND COSMIC, JOIN forces to manifest. You don't make it happen alone. Accepting that you're more than human includes a genuine relationship with the 'mysteries,' and the Creator. You're not required to understand how manifestation works, only to have faith that it does.

Manifestation, the ability to create your world, requires work. You, like other human beings on Earth, participate in the shaping of reality with the help of universal consciousness. If you desire to step forward in your evolution, support is there for the asking. Synchronicity, harmony, and miracles abound when you're willing to do the groundwork. My faith began at age eleven.

My family rarely had extra cash for anything other than necessities. I'd outgrown a hand-me-down bicycle, and we had no money for a larger one. My dad had enrolled my older brother and me in Highlander Boys, a Denver-based, paramilitary organization. Wearing uniforms of black shoes and pants, white shirts, and black ties, we learned to march carrying wooden rifles.

Early in December, the Highlander Boys decided to raise funds by selling holiday cards. Three new bicycles on display at their headquarters would be awarded for the highest sales. The second-place, expensive, red bike had streamlined fenders, a cool light, shiny reflectors, a chain guard, and a real leather seat. It was perfect and exactly my size. The moment I laid eyes on it, I fell in love, and said aloud, "That one's mine."

The boy standing next to me scoffed at my words. "Not a chance. The older guys use their family business to sell the cards. They always win."

My family didn't have a business. My dad worked as a carpenter on a variety of sites around Denver. I couldn't get the image of that bicycle out of my mind. I pored over some possibilities and finally hatched a plan. When the holiday cards became available, I signed out far more boxes than I could carry and piled them in the back of Dad's Ford station wagon. My neighborhood sales were brisk, and by having success as well as failure, I soon discovered the right question to ask potential buyers.

The week before Christmas, I asked Dad to take me and my cards to a carpenters' union meeting at the Carpenter's Hall. During a break, Dad walked me up to the stage, handed me the microphone, and whispered, "Sell some cards, Son."

I looked down at the rugged crowd of men talking and milling about the room. I was nervous but determined. "Hi, everyone."

Most men didn't even look up, but one voice cut through the chatter. "Who are you, kid?"

"I'm Jerry, and my dad is Bob DeSpain. I want to win a prize by selling Christmas cards to all of you, tonight."

"What's the prize?" the same man asked.

My smiled widened as my words got louder. "The best red bike you've ever seen. It has white stripes on the fenders and a mirror and a black leather seat!"

The room got quieter as several men turned toward to the stage. "Don't you already have a bike?" asked another guy.

"I do, but it was my brother's bike, and I'm too big for it now. I need a new one."

Standing on the floor below, my dad waved his hand and caught my eye. I leaned down and listened to him. "C'mon, Son. Ask the big question, the one you practiced all the way here."

"Right," I said, then stood up, took a deep breath, paused, and spoke to those men with conviction. "Why should you buy Christmas cards?"

"I don't know," someone shouted. "Why should I buy Christmas cards from you?

"Because you care!" I yelled. "How many of you care?"

One carpenter stepped forward and said, loud enough for everyone in the room to hear, "I care, kid. How much do they cost?"

I sold a bunch during the break, but by the end of the evening, I'd gotten rid of every single box. The new red bike made for a happy Christmas, indeed.

### The Five Aspects of Manifestation
1) Imagination
2) Faith
3) Clear Intentions
4) Work
5) Gratitude

### Manifestation begins with imagination.
Travel to the countryside and gaze into the night sky.

You'll see perhaps, 2,500 shining stars. According to astronomers, there are *80 million times* more than that in our Milky Way galaxy alone. And an estimated 100 billion more galaxies in our universe! Space is big. So is your imagination.

"Logic will get you from A to B," Albert Einstein said. "Imagination will take you everywhere."

I imagine the Creator as my partner, working together with me on every project. Once I have an initial desire, I begin to "see" possibilities, but I trust my feelings more than my mind. Logic can wait. Deciding to move forward, I sit quietly in a meditative space and balance my breath. When the feeling of unity arrives, the Creator is listening. We breathe together. I make an internal statement. "I wish to…" I trust the feelings my desire creates and imagine the first steps required to bring the desire into reality.

**Faith in oneself is fundamental.**
You've earned this expansive gift called life. Faith in the Creator implies faith in yourself. Faith is an irrational belief because it can't be tested using the scientific method. Belief is based on verification. Newton believed gravity existed before he proved it scientifically. We can't prove the Creator exists, nor should we try. The mystery must remain.

"The cosmos is within us. We are made of star stuff," wrote Carl Sagan, the famed astronomer, and scientist. "We are a way for the universe to know itself."

**Clear intentions gain results.**
The universe can't do your whole job for you. You have intelligence and choice. When you state your desires with clarity, the Creator listens. A clear intention is, "I want to win the red bicycle." A muddy intention is, "I

hope to win."

"Ask, and it will be given to you; seek and you will find; knock, and the door will be opened to you."— Matthew 7:7. Make sure you ask clear questions, seek specific goals, and knock on the right doors.

**Work is required.**
Knowing what you want to manifest, and being willing to do the work necessary, brings results. The Universe supports you as you take the next step in your evolution. Doubt, difficulties, and failures will occur. You're human, and nobody is perfect. The key is to learn from failure and continue forward towards success.

An easy success is to manifest a desired place to park your car while shopping or going out for dinner. My friends have often heard me say, "Dear Gladys, full of grace, help us find a parking place."

It may seem silly, but by stating the desire aloud and asking for help, the space, more often than not, appears. And as I park the car, I always thank Gladys.

The Creator cannot support a desire contrary to your evolution. If you embark on an adventure and discover too many closed doors, it may be time to re-evaluate. If your desire aligns with your evolution, and you take the right action, you'll have support.

I spent a year working on the concept of the television show, "Pleasant Journeys." I shared my vision with trusted friends and listened to their questions and reservations. Understanding the value of clarity, focus, and brevity, I wrote a two-page proposal. A week later, I reduced it to two paragraphs and began to rehearse. When I felt I was sufficiently prepared, three friends acted as program directors that would make the final thumbs-up-or-down decision. Once they'd heard me out, they agreed I was ready.

After making four separate appointments, I met the first program director on my list. "No," he said firmly. "You'd need puppets, music, and other people as characters. It's an old-fashioned and pricey concept. I'm not interested."

Three days later, the next director shut me down and out. "It won't work, and I don't see you as an on-camera personality. It's about charisma. You either have it or not."

The third director was kind and receptive, but, but, but… "I like your idea, but we're a Public Broadcasting station. I'm sorry, but we can't afford it."

After King-TV rescheduled our meeting twice, I began to doubt that my vision would happen. I went to the university bookstore to search for a book, and instead found the Creator's offer of encouragement.

**Gratitude makes you happier.**
"Cultivate the habit of being grateful for every good thing that comes to you and give thanks continuously."—Ralph Waldo Emerson.

To affirm all that is good in life feels right. To offer appreciation to others, and to the universe, is as natural as breathing. The gift of life, manifestation, and joy is a blessing. And you are blessed.

Modern psychologists recognize gratitude as an important human emotion leading to a sense of well-being. Grateful people are happier people.

And because happiness affects health in powerful positive ways, I often say aloud, "Thank you, Creator, for all that is good, all that is right, and all that we create together. I am blessed. And so it is." The universe conspires with your imagination, faith, intention, work, and gratitude. And it feels *divine*.

～ ～ ～

# Listen

## CHAPTER SIX

*Never miss
a good chance
to shut up.*

~Will Rogers~

# The Silent Debate

## Italy

IN THE SPRING OF THE YEAR 1498, Pope Alexander VI called upon one-hundred priests for an assembly in the Sistine Chapel of Vatican City, an independent city state enclave within Rome. When the priests were seated, Pope Alexander got right to the point and announced the reason for the meeting. "Brothers, I am being pressured by several city consuls to banish all Jews from Rome, just as Emperor Claudius expelled them 1,500 years ago."

A rumbling from the audience ensued, followed by the voice of an elderly Venetian priest. "I beg your pardon, Most Holy Father, but won't the Jews rise up in protest?"

"I'm certain they'll be unhappy," sighed the Pope, "but we will have to see what happens. To appease these city consuls, I must issue the decree immediately with an effective date of three months from today."

This decision weighed heavily on Alexander because it was in direct contrast to his previous actions. After Spain enacted the Edict of Expulsion in 1492, some nine thousand impoverished Iberian Jews had arrived at the Papal State's border. Alexander welcomed them into Rome and declared they would be "permitted to lead their lives, free from interference from Christians, to continue their own rites, to gain wealth, and to enjoy other privileges." Historically the Romans had favored the Jews. They didn't push their religion onto others; they were well-connected throughout the empire; and above all, they paid their taxes. Alexander felt the city consuls were petty, greedy, and jealous of the Jew's success. As expected, when news of the decree hit the streets, the Jewish community protested vehemently.

"It isn't fair! Does Pope Alexander think he's the emperor now?"

"This is not right. Rome is our home!"

"The decree is neither holy nor humane!"

An assembly of rabbis met in the synagogue to discuss this outrage and how to respond. After an hour of heated exchanges and disagreements on a plan of action, the room fell into silence. One man stood and addressed the sullen group.

"As some of you know, I am Rabbi Rashi from Paris, here in Rome writing a commentary on the Talmud. The French have learned how to deal with this eccentric man. Alexander likes to gamble and negotiate. He takes risks. What kind of a deal could we make with him?"

After a few minutes of head scratching that was almost audible, one rabbi yelled, "I propose a debate on religion! If we win, we remain in Rome and live in peace. If we lose, we fight."

"Hmm. Excellent idea. We Jews are quite good at debating, aren't we?" Rashi narrowed his eyes and stroked his grey goatee. "And what specific premise shall we suggest for the debate?"

Another rabbi spoke. "The pressing issue at hand is

clear. People of different religions should be allowed to live together in the same city!"

Everyone agreed. It took a week of negotiations with the papal court to make the deal. Pope Alexander consented to a religious debate with a member of the Jewish community the following week and to the terms of its outcome. If the Pope won, the Jews would leave Rome. If the Jews won, they could stay.

At their next assembly, the local rabbis urged Rabbi Rashi to champion their faith and their cause.

"Oi vey, not me," Rashi said, raising both palms to the group. "I am a foreigner here. I cannot speak with authority for your community. Which one of you has the chutzpah to take on this task?"

The roomful of rabbis looked around at each other while trying to be invisible. The cost of losing the debate was too great, and so was the potential damage to their personal reputations. The synagogue was quiet except for a resounding conversation in the back.

After considerable persuasion and coaxing from those around him, a short elderly rabbi named Ezra struggled to his feet. He spoke loudly because he was practically deaf. "I will challenge this imperial Pontiff, but I won't hear him unless he shouts." Ezra shrugged his shoulders and threw up his hands. "Can you picture our stately and most holy goy in his majestic robes screaming at a little ol' nebbish like me?"

All the rabbis laughed heartily.

"Wise Rashi," Ezra requested. "Please make this demand of my opponent. It must be a silent debate."

Rabbi Rashi met with Pope Alexander to negotiate a situation acceptable to both sides. Upon hearing the proposal, the Pope agreed at once. A silent debate, Alexander thought. How quaint. This could be fun and serve my needs as well. God will lead me to victory.

On the day of the great debate, hundreds of people gathered at the Vatican in the courtyard of the Apostolic Palace. Pope Alexander, regally attired in his bulbous silver and gold crown, a dark maroon cape, and ruby-encrusted slippers, perched on his monumental throne. An elegant, marble-topped table holding a wafer and glass of red wine was within his reach.

Wearing a thin, white cotton kittel, a black cloth kippah to cover his head, and leather sandals, wizened Ezra sat on a three-legged wooden stool in front of His Holiness. At the stroke of noon, the debate began.

Alexander stared down at Ezra over the crook in his lengthy nose.

Ezra stared back and didn't blink his eyes for a full minute. The assembled crowd barely breathed.

Alexander abruptly raised his right hand and displayed three fingers.

Ezra quickly responded by raising his right hand displaying one finger and moved it a few inches towards Alexander.

Alexander, his three fingers still in the air, waved his arm in a large circle above his head.

Ezra straightened his arm and aggressively pointed to the ground with his finger.

Alexander reached for the wafer and wine, and held them up, one in each hand.

Ezra paused with a quizzical expression on his face, then pulled a juicy red apple from his pocket.

Alexander shook his head in amazement, rose, and surrendered. "I give up. This man is brilliant. The Jews can stay."

A loud cheer arose from the Jewish onlookers.

Later that afternoon in the Pope's private chambers, the Archbishop asked Alexander what he had been thinking during the debate.

"First," said Alexander, "I held up three fingers to represent the Trinity—the Father, Son, and Holy Spirit. Old Ezra held up one finger to illustrate that both Catholics and Jews believe in the same God. Then I waved my fingers around my head to show that God watches over all of us. Ezra pointed to the ground to show that God not only watches over us, but is always with us, here and now. I held up the wafer and wine to demonstrate that God forgives us our sins. He took an apple from his pocket to remind me of original sin when Adam and Eve were thrown out of the Garden of Eden. That old genius had an answer for everything. Have the Jews sinned because their beliefs are a little bit different than ours? No. God had silently spoken through me, and I had to concede."

That evening the rabbis converged on the synagogue to celebrate their triumph.

Rabbi Rashi kissed Ezra on both cheeks, then spoke close to his ear. "Mazel Tov, Ezra, my mensch! You have saved the day. But how? What were you thinking?"

"Ay-yay-yay! It happened so fast! A quick silent schmooze, and it was over. He starts with three fingers saying we have to leave Rome in three months. I hold up one finger saying that not even one of us is going. Then he waves around his fingers saying all of Rome would be cleared of Jews. I wag one finger at the ground saying we're staying right here." Ezra grinned wickedly. "I threw in a few more silent words that he couldn't hear."

"And then…" prodded Rashi, "what happened during the last argument?"

"Oh, the big finale," chuckled Ezra. "His Holy Popeness gets hungry and grabs his lunch. I think we we're just taking a little break. I feel like having a bit of nosh, too, so I pull an apple out of my pocket."

"Praise be to God!" exclaimed Rabbi Rashi. "Three thousand years ago He led us out of Egypt, and today He allows us to remain in Rome!"

~ ~ ~

# The Tournament

## Colorado Springs, Colorado, April 1963

WHEN SOME FOLKS GET NERVOUS, their hands sweat or heart pounds. Others have tense muscles or feel nauseous. When I get nervous, my bladder commands my legs to trot me to the toilet. Now. Unfortunately, as we neared Colorado Springs for a college debate tournament, I was in a car. The time was seven thirty on a Saturday morning, and we'd been travelling since five.

"I have to pee."

"Jeez, Jerry! We're not even there yet," said my partner Pete in the back seat.

Pressing my knees together to restrict any leakage, I pleaded with the driver, our debate coach. "Can we stop soon, Corky? *Please?* I gotta go."

Corky was more like a favorite uncle than a college instructor. He pulled off the main road into the first driveway to the picturesque entrance of the Broadmoor Hotel, the historical *Grande Dame of the Rockies*.

"This is a great hotel, boys," Corky said as he parked the car. "My wife and I honeymooned here five years ago. Put on your new sports coats and walk in like you belong there."

I threw on mine and ran through the majestic front entryway. Pete strolled. I spotted the restroom sign and trotted briskly through the brightly lit, luxurious lobby with leather sofas and chairs, massive fireplaces, and immense bouquets of colorful blossoms. Tall, leaded glass windows framed the Rocky Mountains in the distance. Inhaling the refined air of one of Colorado's finest hotels, I only sought the odor of the men's room.

Pete finally joined me at the old-style porcelain bank of urinals, and I sighed, "Wow."

"Double wow." Pete was a 19-year-old country boy from Wyoming and about as sophisticated as me, which isn't saying much.

"This is sweet," I said.

"A lot better than the cheap motel Corky lined up for us tonight."

The restroom's carved oak door swung open, and Corky rushed in to relieve himself. "Today's the big day! You boys nervous?"

"A bit," Pete said casually.

He seemed fearless. I was still in awe. "I'm glad the Air Force Academy is sponsoring the tournament. I've always wanted to see what's on the other side of all that fence."

As the three of us met at the marble sinks to wash our hands, Corky got serious. "You'll probably be up against The Dreadnaughts, those two women from the University of Colorado. You know, dreadnaughts like those old British battleships with all their deadly cannons. They haven't lost a *single* debate in the past year. They love blowing their competition right out of the water."

"We know about 'em." Pete smirked and looked over at me. "Dread?"

"Not!" I answered.

"Find their weakness and destroy!" That was Pete's motto.

I mirrored his with mine. "Surprise equals defeat!"

With a wide smile, Corky put his arms around our shoulders and looked at his team in the enormous mirror facing us above the sinks. "The final tournament of the season. Who's gonna win?"

Without hesitation, we spoke in unison. "We are."

Let's travel back a couple of years before this tournament. Pete had been a Wyoming state high school debate champion and was granted a debate scholarship at Adams State College in the southern Colorado town of Alamosa. After high school, I'd labored on construction sites to save up money for tuition, fees, books, food, and shelter.

Three weeks into my first college semester, while sitting in my dorm room at Adams State, I heard a loud voice bellow in the hallway. "Does anyone have public speaking experience?"

I poked my head out the doorway and saw a fellow freshman of average height with short blonde hair, freckled face, and keen blue eyes. An athletic build added to his bold voice. "Are you a debater?" asked the anonymous face.

I chuckled. "Nope. I've been a *masturbater*, but not a *de*bater."

"Oh, I see... a smart ass.".

"But..." I smirked. "Maybe I could learn to be a master debater."

"Ah, funny, too. I like your voice. You could be on the radio. How 'bout public speaking? Any experience?"

"I like public speaking! I was in a bunch of school

plays and musicals in high school. And I was selected to attend a Colorado Boys State program to learn about politics. We even went to the state capital building and watched them talking about passing a bill."

"Talking? That's almost debating right there. We need to talk more."

I gestured dramatically towards my dorm room. "C'mon in."

Pete plopped on the bed and explained his dilemma. "The debate club doesn't care much for freshmen. They're all juniors and seniors, and I don't want to team up with any of 'em. I'm on my own, but I can't do it alone. I need a partner. You interested?"

"Well…"

"And there's one more debate scholarship up for grabs."

That grabbed my interest pronto. "What? A scholarship? Keep talking."

"If you want, I can teach you the basics of debate, but we only have three days."

"Three days?" My chin backed up against my neck.

"Yeah, three days from now. We'll have a debate with the senior team this Friday night. If we do well, you'll get the scholarship."

"Are you kidding me? Tuition, books, and fees?"

"All three. Free."

"Teach me," I said.

"Okay, here's the lay of the land." Pete settled in on the bed with his hands clasped behind his head. "A college debate consists of two, two-person teams—one team on the affirmative side of the issue statement and one on the negative."

"That sounds like me talking to my parents, but I didn't have a partner."

"You got it. And we both need a partner. The debate

lasts one hour on a predetermined topic. For example, it could be, *Resolved: That weapons of mass destruction are useful tactics in a war.*"

"Like *Resolved: That supporting your child's career decision is beneficial for everyone?*"

"Funny again," Pete said. "Good luck resolving that one. So, the first affirmative speaker gets ten minutes at the podium, followed by the first negative speaker for the next ten minutes. Then the second affirmative speaker has ten minutes, followed by another ten from the second negative speaker."

"I like this. When you debate your parents, you only get ten seconds if you're lucky."

Pete nodded in agreement. "I think we have the same parents. After those forty minutes, it's time for rebuttals which are only five minutes each. That's when you refute their argument with contrary evidence, or heck, just a better argument. And the order of speakers switches. The first rebuttal is the first negative, first affirmative follows, etcetera. The final speaker is the second affirmative, because every debate begins and ends with affirmative arguments. The timekeeper keeps the participants on schedule, and one or more judges decide which team wins."

After listening carefully to the format, the debate strategies, and extensive research required, I had two words for Pete. "I'm in."

We woodshedded for three days gathering information and getting me up to speed. Friday arrived too early, and my bladder was working overtime. All eight members of the Adams State College debate team sat up front in the aged and poorly lit classroom. Pete and I sat together mentally running through our facts and tactics. Our opponents were two other Adams State debate team members, both seniors with a 65% win-record. Coach Corky, in the role of Judge Corky, sat in the back with notebook in hand. The topic of the year and on that day was *Resolved: That labor organizations should be under the jurisdiction of anti-trust legislation.*

I hadn't learned much about anti-trust legislation in three days, but with a memorized script provided by Pete, I stood at the podium as the first affirmative speaker, and laid out three comprehensive arguments.

Bill, the first negative speaker, followed me and attempted to undermine the points I'd raised.

Listening carefully to Bill's arguments, Pete wrote copious notes. Then he took his place at the podium in the role of second affirmative. Besides analyzing and spelling out the weakness of Bill's commentary, Pete went on to make two more solid points for our team.

Jules, the flustered second negative speaker, now had to deal with five arguments, but only had time to focus on the three points I'd made.

Partner Pete slipped me his yellow pad to help me with my final task, a brief affirmative rebuttal. Back at the podium, I glanced at Pete's notes and began. "Let's explore what our worthy opponents have most seriously objected to…" Remaining calm and fluid while offering occasional, knowing smiles, I sounded authoritative, just as Pete had taught me.

The moment that hour-long debate ended, Corky delivered his judgement. "Affirmative wins, no question!"

After discussing the highs and lows of the debate with everyone in the room, Corky asked me, "How many years did you debate in high school?"

I lied. "Two years, sir."

"Well, you were amazing. The scholarship is yours, Jerry. Welcome to our club!"

Near the end of that first college year, I told Corky

the truth about my lack of prior experience. Two years of drama and public speaking, maybe. Years of debate experience? Zero. But considering that Pete and I had achieved a 70%-win record—highest of any freshman team recorded in the Adams State chronicles—Coach Corky forgave me.

For the next year and a half, we toured Colorado and its neighboring states debating other colleges in many cities. And we continued to win. Because we were experts at misleading or distracting our opponents, other teams christened Team Pete and Jerry with a new nickname—The Red Herrings.

"Find their weakness and destroy!

"Surprise equals defeat!"

During the spring of our sophomore year, our final debate was the tournament at the Air Force Academy in Colorado Springs in 1963. Only sixteen teams, the best in the five-state area, were invited to compete in an elimination tournament comprised of four rounds of debates: round one has eight debates; round two, four debates; round three, two debates. In the final round, one debate between the two remaining teams. The 1962-63 debate topic had been announced many months earlier. *Resolved: That non-communist nations of the world should establish an economic community.*

The Red Herrings was the only sophomore team invited to the tournament and were not considered contenders to win. The other fifteen, two-person teams were seasoned veterans and primarily college seniors.

High school debate champion Pete was the brains behind our team, and his confidence had been built on experience. I was the clever one, researching and gathering treasure troves of obscure facts regarding the debate topics, which we used to fluster and confound our opponents.

Coach Corky had earned a nickname, too. The year prior, we'd begun calling him "Mr. Bouncy" because of his excitable temperament. He'd raise the volume of his high-pitched voice and gesticulate wildly with hands and arms while bouncing up and down on his feet. He was a good guy, a family man growing a little plump as he skirted middle age—smart, decent, easy to travel with, and the provider of my scholarship.

That Saturday morning in the men's room at the Broadmoor Hotel, Mr. Bouncy was hollering like a cheerleader. "Only sixteen teams, the best in five states, the Air Force Academy, and you guys! Whatever happens today, I'm proud of you."

"You know," Pete said, "we've never experienced an elimination tournament."

"Hey, every debate has elimination. You lose, you're eliminated. Tell you what. Win the tournament, and you'll sleep here tonight."

"Where? In the men's room?" Pete asked. "I mean, who can afford this place?"

"It's the end of the season. There's just enough money left in the team account. You win, and I'll get you guys a room."

That sounded almost sounded too good to be true. "Promise?"

Corky looked me in the eye. "Promise."

"We'll win," Pete declared.

"Let's do this," I said.

We hopped into the car, drove to the Air Force Academy, registered, and convened in the hallway outside the classroom where our debate would take place.

"You're up against Brigham Young University," Corky announced after a tournament official had handed him the first-round schedule. "You guys are on the negative."

"Good," said Pete. "Those Mormon boys hate serious challenges. They like everything copacetic."

"Actually, you met them once in Salt Lake City, early in the season. They beat your butts."

"I remember," I said. "We didn't distract them from the main argument."

"Right," Pete said, "our tactics were wrong. No red herrings today."

As usual, I had an appointment in the toilet. "I have to pee."

"Naturally," Pete replied.

The debate began at 9 a.m. sharp. An hour later, the two judges split their vote, but we edged out Brigham Young with points. Pete and I high-fived while Corky bounced. Adams State and seven other teams remained in the battle.

The bouncing stopped when the official hand Corky the schedule for Round Two. "Good news, boys. You're on the affirmative. The bad news? It's the host team."

"Ah, the mighty Air Force," Pete said. "I've always wanted to debate them. They'll be brainy."

"And rigid," I added. "The tight uniforms look good, but don't allow much room to breathe, let alone think out of the box."

"Red herrings?" asked Corky.

"That's our name," Pete said with a smile. "Time to fling a few at the flyboys,"

The debate began at 10:30 a.m. and ended with a three-judge decision, two to one. We won again. Only four teams remained in the running.

Mr. Bouncy was beside himself, beaming with happiness. "Two up, two down, and two to go!"

Pete's hand went from a victory punch above his head to his stomach. "I'm hungry! Let's get lunch."

The cafeteria buzzed with the defeated debaters proclaiming unfair treatment. Feelings were fragile in this final tournament for senior teams. I heard weeping from the University of Texas duo, one guy and a girl. She wasn't the one crying.

The four remaining teams were The University of Colorado, Southern Illinois University, The University of Arizona, and Adams State College—two sophomores dressed in matching, hunter-green sports coats. The week before, I'd bought them on sale at J. C. Penny and thought they looked smart. I was still a country boy with little real-world experience.

As we returned our empty lunch trays, Pete elbowed me in the ribs. "Let's drop by the Dreadnaughts' table and say hi."

"They'll ignore us."

"Probably."

"Let's go."

The Dreadnaughts' clothing, elegant and severe, suited them. Polished gray blouses complemented their navy-blue, corporate-style skirts. "Dreadful" Susan's long red hair imprisoned in a dense bun hinted propriety. Her thin, painted, ruby-red lips silently spoke danger. "Naughty" Nancy's auburn locks flaunted an imitation of Jacqueline Kennedy's popular pillbox bob. The single strand of pearls on her bony neck trumpeted nobility. Like the powerful attorneys they probably dreamed of becoming, they sat erect, haughtily observing the peons and delinquents tainting the room while eating daintily, so as not to spoil their attire. As we approached their table, I heard Susan say, "Oh, god! It's those green toads from Adams State."

"Ladies," gushed Pete, "congratulations on making the final four!"

"It wasn't difficult," snipped Nancy. "Is this your

*first* major tournament?"

"Yes, it is," I said. "And we feel fortunate to be here."

"As you should," sneered Susan. "I'm surprised they invited such a small school."

"Well, good luck, my fair ladies," offered Pete with a slight bow, "in your next debate."

"You think we need luck?" demanded Nancy.

Susan exploded. "Leave us!"

Chuckling, Pete and I strolled out of the dining hall.

Round Three began at 1 p.m. Our opponents from the University of Arizona were on the affirmative team and took the podium. We listened intently to their opening statements.

As their first speaker sat down, I whispered to Pete, "RGR?"

"No. Not yet. Save it."

RGR was our secret code for "Russia's Gold Reserves." Several months earlier, I'd come across a chart in a three-year-old *U.S. News & World Report* magazine that presented figures for the gold reserves of the world's major nations. It was a solid fact that could also be used as a red herring to engage or distract.

The Round Three decision did not come immediately. The judges argued among themselves and then asked everyone to leave the room.

From the people milling around in the hallway, we learned that the Dreadnaughts had won the other third-round debate between the University of Colorado and Southern Illinois University. Corky, Pete, and I—three bundles of frayed nerves—awaited the result. Ten endless minutes later, a tournament official appeared and announced, "By three votes to two, Adams State College!"

"You're in the final debate!" Corky shouted and

continued chattering congratulations. My bladder interrupted him. "I gotta pee."

"I gotta pee too," Pete echoed.

Ten minutes before the final round, we convened in the spacious science auditorium. The floor in the front was the stage. A broad circle of light illuminated a podium in the middle and two, six-foot wooden tables a few feet behind on each side. Slanting up from the stage, the rows of individual seats easily accommodated the hundred observers—the losing teams, their coaches, several young men in uniform, and a smattering of relatives and fans. Seven judges sat third-row center with an empty chair between each one of them, about eye level with a speaker standing at the podium. The table on the left was for the affirmative team, Adams State College. The table on the right for the negative team, the University of Colorado.

Pete and I took our places at the left table near the double-door entrance to the auditorium. We set down our "brainboxes"—metal recipe boxes packed to the max with note cards containing a myriad of facts and figures we'd researched and gathered throughout the year, along with a handful of recent magazines typical of college debaters: *Time, Life, Newsweek,* and *U.S. News & World Report.*

The debate was scheduled to begin at 3 p.m. The hands of the clock on the wall now pointed to 2:57. Our opponents hadn't shown, and a debate can be forfeited due to tardiness. The audience grew restless. Checking their watches, the judges began to confer.

At precisely 2:59 p.m., the doors swung open. Led by three minions lugging their goods, the Dreadnaughts waltzed in like royalty with noses elevated above the peasants. Eyes riveted on the spectacle unfolding, the audience gasped. One assistant pushed a sturdy library cart filled with heavy tomes. The other two schlepped armloads of news magazines. Expressing disdain as they passed in front of us, the women marched pompously to their side of the room and sat while their assistants arranged their materials.

I was astounded. I think my eyes were wider than my head.

My partner seemed cool and collected as if he could see into the future. "Don't respond," he warned.

I followed his lead and took a few deep breaths. As I stood to take my place at the podium, Pete lowered his head and looked me in the eye. "RGR."

I nodded back with conviction. "Definitely. Surprise!"

"Equals?"

"Defeat!"

Smoothing the lapels of my sports jacket, I walked to the podium, set down my note pad, and addressed the audience. "We are honored to be in this tournament and look forward to debating the fine women of the University of Colorado. My arguments for non-communist nations to establish an economic community center on the creation of strong nation-to-nation relationships which allows labor and financing to move freely between countries. A major benefit will be the prevention of future wars. Nation states working together are unlikely to risk defeating each other. Our opponents might argue that the current communist threat is too great, that with the Soviet Union's vast territory and resources, they'll defeat all attempts to create a world-wide, non-communist, economic community. Thus, I'd like to bring something new, a fresh perspective to this afternoon's contest not heard for the entire season—"

I was interrupted by a resounding snort from Susan

and a lusty snicker from Nancy heard by everyone in the room. I smiled and continued. "In fact, Russia's gold reserves are much less than the combined reserves of the other countries we'll be discussing—"

A malicious cackle erupted from the Dreadnaughts as unrest spread throughout the auditorium.

I kept going. "We'll prove our arguments beyond a reasonable doubt. Here are our main points..." I concluded my affirmative remarks and returned to my seat, feeling the tension vibrating in the room.

"It's gonna get nasty," Pete whispered. "Don't let it get to you."

"I won't."

Stern Susan glared at us while strutting to center stage and then slammed her yellow legal pad on the podium. She spoke with the resolve and nerve of a designated executioner. "My colleague and I are pleased to be in this final round, and we wish to thank all seven judges for their participation. I'd be the last person to accuse our opponents of making up facts in a desperate attempt to win, but the misguided young sophomores from Adams State College, *not even a university*, would have you believe that a vital fact, such as the one they've mentioned, would go unnoticed by *every experienced debater* for an entire season. We trust they'll learn from their mistake."

Pete gave me a gentle tap, fist to shoulder. We watched Coach Corky smirk during a personal minibounce in his chair in the audience. He knew his team and their arsenal of hidden facts.

Susan concluded her arguments with a dismissive sniff and glided back her table as if the case against our arguments had been signed, sealed, and delivered.

Second Affirmative Pete, magazine in hand, ambled to the podium and spoke with composure and authority. "I'm surprised our opponents find fault with our research… and they've called us liars in the most important debate of our careers. Let me dispel *any doubt* that Russia's gold reserves are *far less* than Susan and Nancy would have you believe."

Pete displayed the magazine's cover to the audience. "This is a *U.S. News & World Report* dated April 1960." He turned to the colorful graph. "On page 63, we find an article on the gold reserves held by the world's major nations, accompanied by this chart which reveals that Russia's reserves are far down on the list. As Jerry stated, the current communist threat isn't all that great."

The judges murmured, the Dreadnaughts grumbled, and a whirlwind of whispers engulfed the auditorium.

Pete went on to refute other arguments before his final statement. "In conclusion, I stress once again that *our opponents failed to argue against the facts* about Russia's gold reserves and their diminishing impact on communism, and that failure must stand." He paused. *"And stand strong."*

For most intents and purposes, the debate ended right there, though it officially finished thirty minutes later. The judges asked everyone to leave the room and wait in the hallway for their decision.

Corky, happy but nervous, stood between his two somber bookends as several debaters and coaches showered Pete and me with compliments.

"You guys deserve to win!"

"How'd you keep that gold information quiet for so long?"

"Those women are unbelievable. It was a show, and you showed them!"

Surrounded by teammates and admirers at the far end of the hall, the Dreadnaughts kept to themselves.

It wasn't long before the tournament manager along with the seven judges joined us in the crowded hallway. Everyone grew quiet.

"Five votes to two, the winners are Pete Wyers and Jerry DeSpain representing Adams State College!"

The Red Herrings Debate Team
Right to left—Pete Wyers and Jerry DeSpain

Shouts of "Yes!" soared out of the silence. Amidst the cheers and high fives, Corky put his arms around our shoulders and squeezed us into one being. "I'm so proud of you guys."

With smiles about to rip apart our lips, we shook hands and kept on shaking until Pete asked me, "Where do we go from here?"

Palms and eyebrows raised, I asked the universe, "Who knows?"

As Corky had promised, that night the Red Herrings slept under down-filled comforters on luxurious beds in the arms of the Grande Dame of the Rockies, the Broadmoor Hotel.

The next morning, we returned home to Alamosa with the championship trophy and a hand-lettered certificate declaring our victory. When Corky dropped us off at our apartment complex, he said, "I want you guys in my office Monday morning at 10 a.m."

"Why?" asked Pete.

"I might have a surprise for you."

"I like surprises," I said.

"Just be there. At ten. Sharp."

Pete and I arrived together and on time. Corky's expression looked mischievous, and his wispy hair seemed to be trying to escape from his head. Seated in his chair behind the desk, he was either bouncing slightly or his heart was pounding madly. "Have a seat, you two."

"What's up?" asked Pete.

"I have news," Corky bubbled. "While you two were lounging in the lap of luxury at the Broadmoor on Saturday night, I had dinner with the University of Southern Illinois debate team."

"They made it to the final four," I said. "They must be good."

"They've got a solid program at that school. Anyway, their coach offered me a fellowship to study for my Ph.D. And a job as an assistant debate coach. I've accepted their offer."

We were dumbstruck, but a few words crept out of Pete's half-open mouth. "You're leaving us?"

Before Corky could answer, the phone on the desk rang, and a knowing grin filled his round face. "I think that's for you guys."

Pete answered, listened for a moment, and then held the handset so we could both hear. An unfamiliar voice spoke. "Is this Pete and Jerry?"

"Yes."

"Yes."

"I'm Professor Marvin Kleinau, debate coach at Southern Illinois. I heard you guys on Saturday, and I want to congratulate you on your win."

"Thanks," said Pete.

"That's really nice of you," I added.

"And… I'd like to offer both of you full scholarships to Southern Illinois University, beginning this fall. We want you on our team. And as you probably know, Corky's joining us as well."

"Wow, that's great," replied Pete. "But where's your school? I don't know much about Illinois."

"We're downstate in Carbondale, a small town with a big school. I think you'd like it. What do you think?"

Standing next to each other, almost cheek to cheek, we eyed each other over the phone. Nodding together, Pete and I chanted in unison. "We accept!"

Then, as usual, I had an urgent appointment in the men's room.

~ ~ ~

# Listen Within

*The word listen contains the word silent.*

O NE OF THE GIFTS OF A SPIRITUAL LIFE is silence. In Buddhism, a seeker of light and life is called *shravaka*, a listener. Listening within allows you to hear the Creator. I cherish the feeling of peace and calm arising from stillness.

Filled with chaos and noise, our modern world fails to encourage you to listen within. Televisions, computers, and smartphones with their chats, music, games, and social media create constant distractions. Learning to listen can be quite a challenge. I've been doing it for decades, and I'm still learning. In 1970 I settled into my home base in Seattle, Washington and ended up in Chiang Mai, Thailand in 2017. Trusting my gut, intuition, and Higher Self, I traveled the world while opening my ears and learning to listen within.

## Seattle, Washington and Portland, Oregon

On a glorious Saturday morning in Seattle, I carried flowers, three pieces of fruit, a new handkerchief, and the $75 initiation fee to the house rented by four meditation teachers. Expectant and curious, I was scheduled to be initiated into Transcendental Meditation and given my very own mantra, a word composed of sacred sounds that promised higher consciousness.

Sam, a youthful, 30-year-old recently returned from his teacher training in Mallorca, Spain greeted me at the door. We'd met the week before during two lectures on the benefits of meditation and an hour-long personal interview.

"Are you ready, Pleasant?"

"Let's do it."

"Please leave your shoes at the door and follow me."

Sam led me to a private room at the rear of the house with an altar covered by a bone-white cloth adorned with incense, candles, rice, flowers, and a picture of Maharishi Mahesh Yogi's teacher, Guru Dev. Two chairs faced the altar. Sandalwood and candlelight teased my senses as Sam recited a text in Sanskrit and then invited me to sit. In a quiet chant, Sam spoke my two-syllable mantra and repeated it again and again. Mimicking him, I said it aloud several times.

"Now close your eyes, Pleasant, and say each syllable mentally, without moving your tongue and lips. Take it inside yourself."

Ten minutes later, I heard, "Open your eyes slowly."

Sam smiled. "How do you feel?"

"Like I'm floating," I whispered.

"Good. Meditate for twenty minutes each morning and afternoon, and you'll find it gets even better."


Four months later, I traveled to a retreat at a Franciscan center outside Portland, Oregon to spend three days with fellow Transcendental meditators. I was assigned a small, monastic chamber, complete with white-washed walls, one tiny window, a single bed, dresser, and a carved-wood Jesus on the cross. That afternoon I sat cross-legged on the bed, closed my eyes, and began my meditation. Opening my eyes twenty minutes later, I felt buoyant.

After dinner, fifty meditators of all colors, ages, and backgrounds gathered in the chapel. Sheila, an experienced teacher, asked us to share our experiences. Several folks spoke of serenity, peace, and heightened awareness; a few expressed frustrations and felt a lack of progress. Three meditation teachers listened, commented, encouraged, and supported.

"Anything else to share?" asked Sheila.

Slowly raising my hand from the last row of pews, I said, "Yes."

"Please come forward, Pleasant, so we can hear you."

I walked to the front and faced my colleagues. "Something happened this afternoon, unlike any of my previous meditations."

"Go on," said Sheila.

"I believe I actually transcended."

"Please share your experience with us!"

"I felt myself rise up and beyond my body, and then heard a voice say, 'You're safe.' I accepted what was happening, and suddenly I was above this building and the grounds, looking down, aware of everyone here. 'Observe,' said the voice within. I felt as if I knew each of you, your stories, your hearts. I continued to rise higher and looked down to see the entire city of Portland. I felt somehow related to everyone. Rising even higher, I saw the curve of the earth from above and felt a connection to millions of people . . . and to the planet itself. The voice spoke once more. 'Time to return.' Downward I floated and gently settled back into my body. I lay down for thirty minutes to recover, and then went to dinner."

Sheila, the other teachers, and the seated meditators had quizzical looks on their faces, but no one spoke.

After a long moment, Sheila said, "Thank you, Pleasant. Does anyone else have something to share?"

No one offered any comments and no discussion ensured. Bewildered by the silence, I walked back to my pew. Soon Sheila told us to get a good night's sleep and the meeting broke up.

As the room emptied, a teacher named Peter sat beside me. "I'm glad you shared."

"It was an extraordinary experience. I still feel the energy. I thought that the group might—"

Peter politely caused me to pause by holding up his hand. "The reason the others didn't, or couldn't respond, is probably because they haven't yet had an experience like yours."

"But I've only just begun to meditate!"

"Yes. And you should be pleased with your success. What's important is the process, not the experience, however minuscule or profound. Just keep meditating twice each day."

"Who do you think spoke to me during the experience?"

"You spoke to you, and I'm glad you listened."

As a storyteller in Seattle, I'd made a decent living for twenty-plus years, but one day awoke with a ragged cough. It's just a cold, I thought. Still coughing two weeks later, I went to the doctor. Due to my beloved city's wet climate, mold had infected my lungs, interfering with my breathing and speaking. The doctor explained that I wouldn't last long if I stayed, and two other specialists confirmed his diagnosis. I was devastated. The mayor had christened me "Seattle's Resident Storyteller." Well-known and respected, I had plenty of work. But I had to survive. Shedding a few tears, I said goodbye to my family and friends.

## Tucson, Arizona and Taos, New Mexico

I moved to Tucson, Arizona during 1994 in hopes of finding relief. It worked. The dry desert heat improved my breathing, but Arizona's schools had little funding for artist's visits. After four years of penny pinching and belt tightening, my bank account was nearly empty. It was time to move on, and the universe revealed the destination to me during a visit to Taos, New Mexico.

In 1998, I was invited to spend a month at the Helene Wurlitzer Artists' Colony in Taos. At that time, I had two pressing priorities. With the deadline looming for my newest collection of traditional stories, *Sweet Land of Story: Thirty-Six American Tales to Tell,* I needed to complete the manuscript. And I had to make a decision about relocating to a new city—one that supported my health and my finances.

Conferring with my Higher Self one morning, I asked aloud, "If it be wisdom, where can I live and thrive in the next period of my life?"

The rest of the day consisted of writing *Sweet Land of Story,* a bike ride into town for lunch with two other resident artists, a swim at the Taos YMCA, and a quiet evening in my adobe house reading fiction. I slept well and had a vision of my future that night.

During my morning shower I recalled my dream in vivid detail.

*Scene One: I'm sitting in the back of a limousine traveling from New York City to Albany, New York with Governor Nelson Rockefeller. We both wore black tuxedos. The dream year is 1976, and we're headed to the ribbon-cutting ceremony for the newly built Empire Plaza, a complex of state government buildings in Albany. Because of my love of art, I've been promised a private viewing of the Rockefeller art collection upon returning to the Big Apple. I'm excited!*

*Scene Two: The Governor and I stand behind a wide red ribbon stretched between two columns. The local press is in force, flashbulbs explode, patriotic music plays, and the crowd of onlookers is exuberant. The Governor is handed a huge pair of scissors, and as Rockefeller begins to make the cut, he looks directly into my eyes and says, "You'll do quite well, here."*

*The Final Scene: The two of us are back in the limousine and returning to New York City.*

"Wait!" I yelled with warm water pounding on my head. "I didn't see the art!"

I'd never been to Albany. Several years before I'd only driven past on the freeway, but while researching the Empire Plaza online, I recognized the exact scenes from my dreamscape—the soaring towers, a water fountain in a wide-open plaza, and an oddly shaped theater called the Egg.

I let the dream go and continued working on my book. Swimming at the YMCA two days later, I experienced a flash of the Albany scene and heard Rockefeller's voice. "You'll do quite well here."

## New Hope, Pennsylvania to Albany, New York

I'd like to say I packed up and moved to Albany straightaway. Instead, friends offered me a long-term stay at little cost, in a beautiful condominium about 200 miles from Albany in New Hope, Pennsylvania. After a year in New Hope, the condo was sold, so once again I followed the dream and lived in Albany for about a year and a half. The state of New York had funding for educational programs, and my school performances picked up dramatically.

## Troy, New York

One afternoon in 2001, I drove eight miles north to Troy, New York on the Hudson River, a post-industrial city fallen on hard times. I entered the City Hall and inquired about possible government, state, and city grants. The City Clerk, a kind, older man asked me, "Have you ever owned property anywhere in the United States?"

"No," I said, "I've always rented."

"So, how's your credit rating?"

"It's okay. I don't have too much outstanding debt."

"What about your income? You can't make too much and still qualify for the grants."

"I doubt I make too much. I'm an artist."

He smiled. "Then you've come to the right place at exactly the right time. Troy is a splendid city and has many grants on offer. Take this information on TRIP, the Troy Rehabilitation and Improvement Program. And here's a list of local banks that support the program. If I were you, I'd meet a few of the locals who care about Troy and know what's going on."

He gave me names and phone numbers, and within a week, I met Sid Fleisher, the unofficial mayor of a small neighborhood in South Troy. Both wise and generous, Sid knew his neighborhood inside and out. After showing me several buildings while discussing their merits and faults, he walked me around an ugly, yellow, boarded-up, three-story brick building perched in the middle of a nice-looking block.

"What's the story here?" I asked.

"Former crack house," he said, "built over a hundred years ago. It's got great bones. The city owns it now, and TRIP will do the rehab. You'd do quite well to have it."

Rockefeller's voice echoed in my head. "You'll do quite well here."

I qualified for the TRIP program, signed a contract for the property, and agreed to live in the neighborhood for fifteen years. After the building was taken down to bricks and studs, then completely remodeled, I moved in. At age 59, I became a bona fide homeowner. With a charming apartment to rent on the first floor, my mortgage was paid for each month.

I considered the building a gift from the universe. I was truly grateful for the comfortable home, and my Troy friends and neighbors, for each of those fifteen years. The sale of the property in 2017 allowed me to retire to Northern Thailand, where I continue to live and thrive.

**How do you learn to listen within?**

As I mentioned before, learning to listen in this bustling, restless world is a challenge. Some habits die hard but create life when they're gone. Start by taking a few simple steps to introduce some silence in your life.

When you get in your car, does the radio immediately blare, spewing out commercials, opinions, tragic news, and hit songs you didn't know were hits?

*Turn off the radio.*

Even when you're not watching it, does your TV in the empty living room blather endlessly to the rug, couch, coffee table, and bookshelves?

*Turn off the TV.*

Are you addicted to your smartphone like a teenager who checks the screen every minute to see if a minute has gone by, or if any friends, relatives, and strangers have posted pictures of what they're eating and where they're dining on Twitter, Instagram, and Facebook? Or are you walking aimlessly while engrossed in the video game Doom on your phone and have just stumbled into a fountain?

*Put down the phone for a while. Really. You can do it. I know you can.*

Are you that person at the party (or anywhere else) who just can't stop talking? The one who asks anyone, "So how's your daughter?" And after they say, "Fine," you launch into "Well, my daughter just graduated from Harvard and married a surgeon and they're living in an amazing mansion except they haven't invited me over yet but I think that…" and then ramble on for ten minutes until your next leading question like "How's work going?" which is followed by ten more minutes about how your work is going?

*Stop talking for a while. Really. Maybe you can do it. I hope you can. Think about these words from the Dalai Lama. "When you talk, you are only repeating what you already know. But if you listen, you may learn something new."*

**Listen to Others**

In the silent debate, Pope Alexander and Rabbi Ezra watched and listened, but didn't hear. They only assumed incorrectly, but fortunately, they both won without losing. Silence, the absence of sound, provides tranquility and peace. Listening to your inner silence and the silence of others can open doors to deeper understanding.

Corky, my college debate coach, insisted we listen carefully during every debate. He explained how debaters engage in competitive listening. While *pretending* to listen, contestants are often planning their rebuttal, and often miss clues that could shift arguments.

"Be attentive throughout the entire debate," Corky insisted. "Listen for your opponent's weaknesses and strengths. Watch their body language. Sit back, relax, and take it all in. You'll be surprised at what you actually hear."

By making a genuine effort to understand the speakers, I listened with an open mind, and later asked questions to confirm I'd gotten the message. Active listening provided The Red Herrings with a high percentage of wins. Give it a try and watch your success in communication improve.

**Higher Self**
Higher Self has many names—intuition, inner wisdom, the Holy Spirit, and Buddha nature. Your Higher Self speaks in a loving internal voice that encourages and looks out for you. Intuition is an instinctive awareness that provides a reliable guide in manifesting your desires. Rooted in your gut, intuition brings inspiration that is beyond your brain. Thinking aids in human evolution but has its limitations. Trust yourself. The Creator celebrates your successes and resulting happiness if you're willing to listen within and act upon what you hear.

**Listen to the Sound of Silence**
The goal of meditation is to quiet and bypass the thinking mind. When you become calm and centered, the inner voice that is you can be heard. Repeating the sacred sounds of a mantra or counting the inhales and exhales of your breath creates the feeling of letting go.

Active meditation works as well. Swimming, running, Thai Chi, yoga, or a walk in the woods can produce meditative states which allow you to hear your inner voice.

After my initiation into Transcendental Meditation forty-six years ago, I shared my excitement with family and friends and encouraged them to sign up. Several did, but only a few stayed with it. Because this method worked for me, I believed that it was the right program for everyone. I now understand that everyone must find the meditation process that suits them.

The Information Age provides a wealth of knowledge, inspiration, and options. Google 'how to meditate,' and you'll get twenty-seven million hits. Talk with (and listen to) your meditating friends and explore your options.

### If It Be Wisdom

When you begin to mediate, or before you sleep at night, or any time you have a question, state your intention honestly and clearly. Guidance about jobs, love affairs, abundance, and spiritual growth benefit from the initial phrase, "If it be wisdom…" This assures the universe that your actions and goals are in the interest of planet Earth and her inhabitants. Your inner wisdom prevails when you align your desires with the greatest good of all. For example:

*"If it be wisdom, how can I overcome my grief?"*

*"If it be wisdom, is _____ right for me at this stage of my life?"*

*"If it be wisdom, what must I understand, let go of, or embrace to continue my evolution?"*

I end my wisdom questions with *"Thank you, God, and so it is."*

Your Higher Self, always present, is the masterful cocreator of your spiritual evolution. Practice, patience, and trust are necessary to hear you speaking to you. Answers arrive in gut feelings, visions, dreams, or a hearty Aha! Listen with your whole being, and you'll hear a voice that is loving, kind, and without doubt.

~ ~ ~

# Courage

## CHAPTER SEVEN

*It takes courage
to grow up and become
who you really are.*

~E. E. Cummings~

# Tossing Eyes

## Venezuela—The Pemon People

ONE DAY BROTHER JAGUAR PADDED DOWN to the beach and saw Brother Crab looking intently out to sea. "What are you watching for, Brother?" asked Jaguar.

"Sister Shark," said Crab. "She's swimming off to the left. I can't throw my eyes into the water if she's about."

"You can throw your eyes out of your head?" Jaguar shook his head in disbelief. "This I must see!" The curiosity of the big cat coursed through his sleek body, but he waited patiently next to Brother Crab.

They made a quite unusual and multi-colored pair perched together on the white, sugar-fine sand. Muscles rippled under Jaguar's orange and beige skin covered with a maze of black spots. Crab was in the Atlantic blue crab family, though his pinchers glistened crimson red and mustard yellow in the sunlight, and his main shell leaned toward a shade of teal in contrast to his azure blue legs. Weighing in at two hundred pounds, Jaguar measured two meters from the tip of his nose to the end of his tail. Compact little Crab had ten crusty legs but was only a bit bigger than one of Jaguar's paws.

After five minutes of intense staring into the crystal-clear water, Crab spoke again. "All right. Shark has gone. Watch closely." Crab popped his eyes from his head, tossed them far out into the ocean, and then broke into song.

*Eyes, oh eyes, fly far away.*
*Then return home and show me what you've seen.*

A few moments later Crab's eyes flew out of the water and back into his head.

"That is stupendous!" Jaguar jumped to his feet; his fur seemed to vibrate with electricity. "Do it for me! Do it for me! Take my eyes out and send them into the sea!"

"Not now, Brother. Patience. Sister Shark has grown curious, and she's swimming this way."

Narrowing his amber cat eyes while raising his burly chest higher, Jaguar glared out at the seemingly serene water. "Jaguar isn't afraid of Shark. I insist that you do it now. Throw my eyes into the sea."

"Okay, Brother Jaguar, but don't say I didn't warn you." Crab sang again.

*Eyes of my brother, fly far away.*
*Then return home and show him what you've seen.*

Jaguar's eyes popped out of his head and flew into the ocean. Suddenly, he realized that he was blind. And scared. "Bring my eyes back now," he growled, "or I'm going to get angry, really angry."

"They're your eyes," Crab said with a shrug. "You call them back."

Jaguar tried but he didn't sing like Crab; he roared.

*Eyes, oh eyes!*
*Far out to sea!*
*Fly home now!*
*Come back to me!*

But his eyes didn't hear, so his eyes didn't obey. Jaguar saw nothing, only a black void. "Help me, Brother Crab," he snarled, "before I devour you."

"Your problem is that you growl and yell and roar. If you sing harmoniously, your eyes will return. Listen carefully to the way I do it."

*Eyes of my brother, far out to sea.*
*Fly home now and show him what you've seen.*

Jaguar's eyes flew from the sea and back into his head. They had seen many exotic visions while they explored the world of water. Jaguar lay on the hot sand, purring and sighing and laughing with delight. Soon he leaped up and stuck his snout in front of Crab's craggy face. "I must see more! Please do it again for me, Brother. Send my eyes back into the sea."

"Now is not a good time. Trust me. Sister Shark may be near."

"Just one more time," Jaguar hissed. "Then I'll leave you alone."

Crab agreed and sang once more.

*Eyes of my brother,*
*Fly far away.*
*Then return home,*
*And show him what you've seen.*

Jaguar's eyes flew out of his head and plopped into the sea. A moment later, they heard a great slurp near the surface of the water. Sister Shark had swallowed them both in one gulp.

Immediately Crab sang for Jaguar's eyes to return, but they didn't come back.

Blind again, roaring with fear and rage, Brother Jaguar pounced toward the sound of the song and scratched at the sand, trying to snag Crab with his sharp claws.

Crab frantically scuttled sideways, then into the ocean to save himself from his raving brother.

Jaguar paced back and forth on the beach, stumbling into holes and bumping into boulders, as his mind paced back and forth in his head. If I can't see, I can't hunt. If I can't hunt, I won't be able to eat. If I don't eat, I'm gonna die. Finally, he lay down and wept.

High in the sky, Brother Condor, the King of the Vultures, sailed round and round the fluffy clouds, barely moving his immense wings that stretched out five feet on each side of his thin body. His beady eyes had been scrutinizing the tiny scene far below, and he wondered what was happening. He circled down and landed next to Jaguar shaking and sobbing on the sand, though no tears fell from his empty sockets.

Once he'd folded his magnificent wings into his body, and ruffled up the white feathers encircling his neck, Brother Condor looked like an ancient priest in regal black robes with a fleece collar. He cocked his deep maroon, featherless head and his dimpled crown tilted down toward Jaguar. "Why do you cry, my brother?"

"Sister Shark has eaten my eyes!" Jaguar bellowed. "I can't see! I can't hunt! And soon I'll starve to death!"

"You are in a bad way," agreed Condor, "but perhaps I can help."

"Yes, oh yes, please," begged Jaguar, his paws pressed together in prayer. "If you can get my eyes back, I'll repay you somehow. I'll hunt game for you! I promise!"

"Let me see what I can do. There may be a way." Brother Condor flapped his wings, rose quickly above the clouds, and sailed over the horizon. Soon he returned with a pot of hard yellow paste from the curi tree. He built a small fire, set the pot on top, and used a stick to stir the melting paste into a soft goo. Brother Condor then spread the hot curi paste into Jaguar's empty eye sockets.

Jaguar recoiled and sprung up, screaming in pain and rubbing his sockets with the back of his paws. "It burns, Brother! Oh, how it burns!"

"Lift up your eyelids now," Condor crooned in a soothing voice. "You must open your new eyes and let them see."

Jaguar obeyed, and the burning stopped. His new eyes glowed with brilliance. He could see better and farther than before. He bowed down his head and spoke from his heart. "Thank you, bless you. I am indebted to you, Brother Condor."

"You're welcome. Now go hunt us something to eat. All this work has made me hungry!"

Ever since then, ages and ages ago, the people of the Pemon tribe say this is why jaguars have such luminous yellow eyes. And, they add, why Brother Jaguar is so generous with the rewards of his hunts and always leaves something extra for Brother Condor.

~ ~ ~

# Strong Heart

*Courage is found in unlikely places.*
-J. R. R. Tolkien-

## Life on Chase Street, Denver, Colorado

MY BROTHER BOB SMACKED INTO ME from behind, nearly knocking the coffee can full of night crawlers from my hand. Bob was fifteen and I was fourteen. I don't know how old the nightcrawlers were, but they didn't have much longer to live.

"Get down!" he whispered. "I think we've been spotted."

I hugged the cold wet grass on the ninth hole green of the golf course as an intense beam of light passed over us.

"I see you, assholes!" boomed the angry manager. "I've already called the cops, so don't even think of running!"

"Run, Jerry, and don't drop the can!"

We jumped up and raced through a nearby thicket of trees. Bob beat me to the six-foot, wooden fence, a hundred meters beyond the woods. Wearing slippery tennis shoes soaked from the early evening rain that brought the night crawlers to the surface, we climbed over the fence one-handed to protect our precious cargo. We retrieved our bikes from their hiding place and rode the two miles back home, infinitely pleased with our escape.

The moment we stepped through the front doorway of our house on Chase Street, Mom exploded. "You're dripping water all over my clean floor! You've missed supper! And oh, my God! Are those worms?"

"Night crawlers," I said proudly.

"Worth a penny each," Bob chimed in.

"Where'd you get them?"

"The new golf course," I said. "It's got acres and acres of grass."

Mom furrowed her brow into a question mark. "And they just let you catch them?"

"Well," stammered Bob, "I don't think they mind."

"If you break the law, we'll all be in trouble. You boys know that! I don't have the money to get you out of jail, so stop making me worry." With a big sigh, she let her arms fall to her sides. "Well... I'm glad you're home anyway. Your dinner's on the stove."

"Okay," said Bob. "We're gonna count tonight's haul before we eat. You look exhausted, Mom. Go to bed if you want. We'll do the dishes."

"Use lots of newspaper on my table. I don't want to see any worm smears in the morning."

We covered the table top with ten layers of newspaper, dumped out both coffee cans, and began the slimy process of pulling the crawlers apart from each other while counting the evening's booty.

"I got 223," Bob said.

"186 here."

One second later, Bob the Math Wiz spoke. "409. Not bad. I'll take them to the bait shop tomorrow. Another couple of bucks for each of us."

"How soon can you buy the car?"

"I need another seventy bucks. Wanna loan it to me?"

"Are you kidding?" I asked. "I'm saving for a car too, ya know."

Hey... I get my license next year. You've got *two years* to go." He smirked and punched me in the arm. "C'mon, buddy. I'll pay you back."

"I know you will, but it ain't gonna happen."

The year before this escapade, my parents had separated. Our father had moved out and remarried. Within a year of their divorce, Mom earned her high school diploma, learned to drive, bought an older, four-door Chevrolet sedan, and got a job filing documents for the county. She showed us how to be strong like her, how to plan and carry on together. Laundry was done on Saturday mornings, and groceries were purchased on Saturday afternoons. Bob, Roger and I helped clean house throughout the week. We made our beds each morning, and then washed and dried the dishes each night.

At age 33, Mom was still strikingly beautiful. Three

men in the neighborhood had asked her out on dates, but she laughed off the proposals. Not to their face, of course. She was too polite for that. They were not her type, and she had the strength, resolve, and patience to wait for Mr. Right, if there indeed was such a man.

Relishing the freedom from our father's strict control, my brothers and I attended school, played sports, and hung out with our friends. When my father lived on Chase Street, the only thing on the wall was a bear-skin rug. He took it when he moved out. Our house had no books, no artwork, nor any music I cared to hear. I felt the need to have some "culture" in life, whatever that meant.

One afternoon I visited the local music store and returned with Wagner's "Ride of the Valkyries" and Hayden's "Trumpet Concerto." They were the first classical compositions to grace Chase Street. Not just our house, probably the whole block.

"That's not my kind of music," Mom said, "but if you like it, good for you."

Bob didn't agree. "Are you nuts? You shoulda bought some rock 'n' roll albums."

Roger didn't comment on my musical taste and escaped outside to play.

I made money doing whatever I could—shoveling snow in the winter, mowing lawns in the spring and summer, pulling weeds from neighbor's gardens. And I tucked away as much as possible into my savings account.

One day, Duane—my best buddy and our paper-boy—rode over to Chase Street on his bike, ready to deliver 110 copies of *The Denver Post* to his customers.

"Want my paper route?"

"You're quitting?" I asked.

"Nope. I'm gettin' another route, and I can't handle

both of 'em.

"I don't know, Duane. What's it like? How big is it? Do you have a map?"

"We don't need a map. C'mon and ride with me. I'll *show* you where it is and how to hit the porches every time."

With the money I'd saved, I bought larger handlebars for my bike, sturdy canvas bags, and became the neighborhood paperboy. It wasn't just a job. It was an official business. I purchased the newspapers from the *Post* management and collected payments from my customers. The difference between the cost of the papers and the money I collected became my profit. If a customer stiffed me, it was my loss. A van rumbled up to my house each afternoon, and the man in the back tossed a heavy bundle of papers on the lawn. Depending on the weather and size of that day's paper, getting them ready took about a half-hour and then another hour for delivery. I'd have to fold 'em, stack 'em, and arrange 'em carefully in my canvas bags. The fold had to be tight and precise, so the papers would fly straight and land intact. Each paper might need a rubber binder, or on rainy days, a plastic sleeve. When my products were ready for the market, I'd ride the route and fling the latest news to my neighbors.

On Sunday mornings, Mom might help me prepare the newspapers, thick with weekend features and ads. One day before dawn, we chatted and worked while we woke up.

"What kind of job would you like when you finish school, Jerry?"

"Teaching, I think. I love English. And I want to travel."

"Where do you want to go?"

"To an island on the other side of the world. It's

called Ceylon, and it's shaped like a giant pearl. Right below India."

"Why there?"

"I read a book last week about Marco Polo and how he traveled all over Asia about 700 years ago. When he got to Ceylon, he said it was the most beautiful island in the world and that the people had skin the color of gold. I got a chill when I read it. I want to see these golden people."

"Honey, you can make that happen. You can do anything you want. Don't let anyone stop you. And tell me the stories when you come home."

"I will, Mom."

I couldn't fit all the papers in the canvas bags hanging down from my handlebars and had to make two or three trips to cover my Sunday morning route. When I'd finished delivering, Mom had breakfast waiting. She truly cared about me.

During the last week of every month, I collected money from my 110 customers. Invoice pad in hand, hair combed, and dressed as neatly as I could afford, I rang doorbells in the evenings. Most people paid me in cash on their front porches and stoops, but not Miss Judy-Peach Benson. I quickly learned to visit her at the *end* of one of my collection nights. Somewhere in her '70s, this sweet, Irish women-of-age dressed for the event each month. Wearing a withered, golden wig, and a patched, brightly colored frock, Judy-Peach would fling open her door the moment she heard my foot hit the porch and greet me with a grin.

"You're here at last. Come in, Mr. Paperboy!"

"Hello, Miss Benson. I'm here to collect."

"I know why you're here, Jerry. Tea first as usual."

She told me tales of the 1930s vaudeville circuit from Los Angeles, San Francisco, Seattle, and Denver.

Forcibly retired by changing tastes, she moved into a vintage house and filled its rooms with mementos of her songstress past. The chocolate-brown, upright piano that Judy-Peach polished each day ruled her living room's grandmotherly décor.

In Judy-Peach's home, the business part of a paper route, and the patience part, played into the profits. If I shared tea, heard a few anecdotes, and took in at least three songs—most of which I'd heard her sing before—I'd leave with a one-dollar tip added to her three-dollar charge for the newspapers. If I only had time for two songs, she cut my tip in half. One song meant twenty-five cents. In the rare instance I didn't join her inside, no tip.

Every time I arrived at Judy-Peach's house, Lipton tea and homemade Irish biscuits awaited. I didn't really care for the tea, but I liked her biscuits. One evening during tea, she wanted to discuss the quality control of my delivery system. "I don't like to complain, Jerry, but the paper ended up on the step, not the porch, two different times this past month. Thank goodness, it was on the highest step. Otherwise I'd have had to bend too far down to pick it up!"

"I apologize, Miss Benson. I promise to do better this coming month."

"Of course, you will, honey. Now eat your biscuits and listen up."

Judy-Peach's arthritic fingers hovered over the keyboard for a moment before she began. As usual as tea and biscuits, she launched into Judy Garland's version of "Somewhere Over the Rainbow," followed by "Tea for Two," "Pennies from Heaven," and "Blue Moon." Her voice held firm on all but the high notes that might stray off pitch. At her advanced age, a bit of wobbling was expected. Harry Belafonte's "Day-O"

(The Banana Boat Song) came next on the agenda, and
Judy-Peach requested that I join in. I summoned my
Customer Service Department and sung along.

*Day-o, day-o*
*Daylight come and me wan' go home*

By the end of the first verse, I definitely wanted to
go home. However, as usual, the *déjà vu* finale could
not be skipped—a rousing rendition of Kate Smith's
seriously patriotic song, "God Bless America" by Irving
Berlin. Outside in the fresh air and silence, I'd had
enough pop culture for the night. Whew, I earned one
extra dollar again as a tiny audience of one.

(For those of you who have never experienced Kate
Smith or her renowned version of "God Bless America," just think of one word: LOUD! Imagine a five-
foot, ten-inch, substantial woman of 235 pounds of
which fifty pounds might have been lungs, belting out
this song to the New York Yankee's baseball stadium
packed with thousands of people, her voice clearly audible to everyone in the general zip code and perhaps
on a few distant planets. For those of you who *experienced* her singing it, listen within. Her voice is probably
still echoing in there somewhere.)

At the end of my first year as a paperboy, I took on a
second job washing windshields at the local Lakeshore
Drive-In Theater. No salary, just tips. With a gigantic
outdoor screen and the capacity to entertain up to a
couple thousand folks sitting in 900 cars and trucks,
the theatre did a brisk business. Customers pulled into
spaces with clear views of the screen and hung heavy,
shoebox-sized speakers inside their vehicles on left
front windows rolled down a bit.

Seven nights a week I arrived at the theatre as dusk
fell during the spring, summer, and fall, ready to clean

pigeon shit from the wooden railings surrounding the outdoor viewing area. For the "privilege" of carrying my bucket of water and ammonia, rags and squeegee to the entry gate, the tight-fisted manager demanded that I ask every arriving driver if I could clean the windshield. "Be polite, and clean as many windshields as possible. Don't ask for a tip, and always say 'thank you' when you get one. And never complain when you're left empty-handed."

Folks drove up to the entry booth, paid for their tickets, pulled their cars or trucks forward, and stopped next to me.

"Wash your windshield?"

"Why not? And loan me one of your rags so I can wipe the inside."

"Yes, sir!"

When I finished a vehicle, the patron rewarded me with a nickel, dime, or occasionally a quarter. About four out of ten were skinflints and offered nothing or maybe only a "Thanks, kid."

After the last vehicle entered for the final showing and the front gate closed at 10 p.m., I rode my bike home in the dark, my pockets jingling with change.

Mom often surprised me by waiting up, tired as she was from work, to help count my earnings. Twelve to fifteen bucks each night added up, and my savings account kept growing.

Brother Bob finally accumulated enough cash to buy a baby-blue, 1949 Ford, two-door coupe. He'd give me a ride to school during the week, but I had to find my own way home. Freedom, sports, and his girlfriend occupied first, second, and third place on his list of priorities. His home presence dwindled to "Morning, let's eat, let's go, and see ya later."

My parent's divorce might have affected brother Roger
more that the rest of the family, because he was a little
younger. One of my father's outrageous antics doomed
any lingering respect we had for him. He took us boys
fishing with one of his rowdy friends. They told us to
get behind a knoll, then took the boat out on the lake,
lit sticks of dynamite, and flung them into the water.
The deafening blasts terrified us, and the explosions
hurled scores of dead or dying fish into the air. They
rained down around the boat, only a few large enough
to eat. After that incident, the word "respect" from our
father's incessant chant—"They may not love me, but
by God, they'll respect me"—meant nothing whatso-
ever.

But brother Roger pulled himself through the hard
times and grew into "the most handsome boy on the
block." That's what one of Mom's friend said. "You'd
better watch out for him, Eleanor. He's going to have
lots of girlfriends." Roger followed brother Bob into
the sport of wrestling and grew strong as well as good-
looking. He studied hard, improved his grades, and
walked and talked with confidence.

Mom's love and strength combined with the absence of our father helped the DeSpain boys become
independent, to accept the necessity of responsibility,
and to learn self-control.

Not a regular churchgoer, Mom began attending
Sunday services at the nearby First Christian Church
and asked us to go with her. Bob said no, I occasionally
agreed, and Roger said, "I'll go when Jerry goes." Sitting together on a pew in the back, Mom often broke
down during the sermons.

When we got home one Sunday afternoon, I asked,
"What's making you cry in church, Mom?"

"I've been praying to God for a good man. Someone

to love you boys, and me. I don't know how much longer I can do all this on my own."

That may have been the first time I'd seen her reveal any hint of weakness. She certainly didn't take any grief from her former husband.

Two months later, Mom met Gene and our world changed. A friendly, reputable neighbor—Gene's sister—introduced them. Gene was tall, handsome, and in excellent shape. He'd lost his beloved wife, Rose, to heart failure two years earlier, and had been raising his 10-year-old son, Greg, on his own.

Gene asked out Mom the following Saturday, and within a month they were dancing at the local American Legion, knocking down pins at the bowling alley, and driving up to Red Rocks Park for picnics.

A few weeks later Mom was whipping up our favorite chocolate cake in the kitchen, a cozy room standard for the '50s—yellow walls and cabinets, white stove and fridge, fading patterns on the linoleum floor. I stood in the dining room looking through open pass-through in the wall, waiting to lick frosting from the spatula.

"Jerry, do you think Gene's a good man?" Her tone told me she felt troubled.

"Yeah, he's a nice guy. And he likes you."

"He likes me?" She stirred the frosting a little faster. "How do you know?"

"He lights up when he talks to you."

"What do you mean, honey?"

"Well, he smiles a lot and kinda glows."

She set down the metal mixing bowl and leaned against the counter. "You're making that up!"

"No, I'm not, Mom. I see what I see." I motioned to the bowl. "And I see the spatula there. I could clean that for you."

She smiled and handed it over. "It's yours. Don't tell your brothers."

"So, do you like him?"

"Yes, I do… but I'm worried. Who in his right mind would take on you three boys as well as me? And bring his son into our family? That's such a risk."

"Maybe he's brave."

"He'd have to be very brave. Maybe stupid and brave."

I felt honored and warm that she trusted me enough to confide in me. "You know, Mom, it's obvious that you like him a lot. You glow when you talk about him."

"I glow?" Mom skin flushed pink. "Oh, Jerry, what am I going to do with you?"

She finished making the cake, and I finished licking the spatula. This had been the first time she'd really talked about Gene. The next morning, she started glowing again at the breakfast table while serving up plates piled with bacon, eggs, and toast.

"Gene calls me 'Ellie.' I like it. And he's one of us. I mean, he grew up here and graduated from Arvada High School, right up the road. He played all kinds of sports and then went into the Army Air Force where he was a physical education instructor and helped get the new recruits in shape."

"Was he a pilot?" Roger asked.

"No, I don't think so."

"How old is he?" Bob asked.

"Ha, he's two years younger than me! Isn't that amazing?"

"What does he do?" I asked. "I mean his job?"

"He's a pet supplies salesman and drives all around Denver, taking orders for pet stores." Mom was in the spotlight, and we were cross-examining her, but she seemed to like it.

"Does he make much money?"

"Oh, aren't you the nosey one, Jerry. He works hard and makes enough."

"What's his religion?" Bob asked.

"He's Lutheran. He attends church nearly every week and wants me to go with him Sunday. I said yes."

"What does he say about us?" I mumbled through scrambled eggs. "About Bob, Roger, and me?"

"Don't talk with your mouth full, please. Gene likes you guys. And he realizes that Bob and you will soon be out of the house with school, marriage, and all."

"Do you love him?"

She finally sat at the table, silent for a moment. "I can't answer that yet. I know he's a good man. We'll see what happens."

Left to right—Greg, Jerry, Gene, Eleanor, Bob, Roger

They married in November 1957 at Redeemer Lutheran Church in Denver Colorado. The little house on Chase Street grew crowded, and we had to share bedrooms. Bob, Roger and I showered at school five days each week, which helped alleviate the daily war over one overused bathroom. Mom quit her job and stayed busy preparing meals, doing errands, and cleaning up after four boys. I can still hear her sewing machine purr as she made shirts and jackets for each of us.

Gene worked at a wholesale pet supply company. He visited pet stores each day, took orders from the managers and returned to the warehouse to pull the items from the shelves. At the end of his shift, he boxed the orders for shipping. He worked hard for five days a week and came home exhausted.

Late on a Friday afternoon I got home from cross-country practice to find Gene sprawled on the living room sofa, his sports jacket draped on the back of the chair, his shoes still on his feet hanging over the end of the sofa. Wearing a cheery apron, Mom came from the kitchen to announce dinner. We both saw that the soles of Gene's shoes had holes in them.

She shook his shoulder lightly. "Wake up, honey."

Gene sat up and rubbed his eyes.

"It's time for dinner, and we're buying you new shoes tomorrow."

"Dinner sounds good, sweetheart, but let's wait on the shoe purchase. We'll pay the electric bill first. I can wear these for another week or two."

This is a different kind of man than I'm used to, I thought. Bob grumbled about the new order of things—that he'd be glad to move out anytime and he was waiting for Gene to call him out on something. In my mind and heart, Gene was polite to everyone and accepted each of our established household roles.

On a Saturday morning about a month later, my new stepdad was halfway through washing his car in front of the house. Brother Bob pulled up in his pride and joy, the Ford coupe, but Gene's car, bucket, and hose extended into Bob's usual parking space. My brother didn't appreciate having his space usurped. He parked in the street, jumped out of his car, walked toward Gene, and yanked the hose out of the bucket. I stood at the mailbox and watched in shock as he twisted the nozzle, and without saying a word, sprayed Gene from face to feet and back up to his head.

Bob stared at Gene—drenched and dripping—daring him to react.

Gene looked bewildered as he stared back, trying to understand what just happened. I watched Gene clench his fists and open them again, one time, two times, three times. His face turned red, and he expelled a deep breath. Not one word passed between them.

Taller than Bob and very fit, Gene had combat training. My stomach churned as I imagined this shaping into a brutal fight.

Suddenly, my stepdad threw his sponge in the bucket, spun away from Bob, and strode into the house. Bob watched Gene go as I crept up next my brother.

"Why?" I asked him in a whisper.

"I'm pissed, all right? And I'm outta here." He jumped into the coupe, slammed the door, drove away with a screech of tires on the pavement.

After changing clothes, Gene returned to finish washing his car. My stomach relaxed, and I began to understand just how different from my father this new stepdad was. The incident passed, and Bob never challenged Gene again. Our crowded household remained in flux, but without rancor.

Gene's ten-year-old son Greg had lived with his grand-mother for the two years after his mother's death but spent time with his dad on the weekends. He found himself challenged with a completely different life on Chase Street. This single child had become the young-est of four brothers. He'd acquired a stepmother and had to share his dad with the rest of us. He'd left his friends behind, and a new, smaller school awaited. Greg survived the transition by being quiet and shy, though observant. He protected his badly bruised heart by keeping his emotions hidden, but his resilience allowed him to be absorbed into the new family life, and before long he became one of the boys.

One dark night a few months later, we four broth-ers were home alone. Bob had banged up his knee and elbow in wrestling practice. He took off the Band-Aid and the wound didn't look good. He sent brother Greg to the corner drug store, three blocks away. On his way back, a stranger leaped from an alleyway, grabbed Greg, and tried to molest him. Greg fought back and escaped by kicking his assailant in the nuts. Beyond scared, he ran home and told us what happened.

Bob went to his bedroom closet, loaded his pellet gun, pumped it, and stood poised for action. "Let's get this guy!"

The four of us ran up and down the alleys in search of the deviant, but fortunately for everyone involved, he was nowhere to be found.

Later in our adult lives, while reminiscing after din-ner, Greg shared how he'd felt during those years in his adopted family. "I had three brothers looking out for me. I felt included. Bob said he'd teach me to wrestle, and Roger said he'd help. I followed them into sports and did well in junior and senior high. It was a turning point in my life."

When I was sixteen, I purchased my first car—a sky-blue, 1952 Chevrolet, two-door sedan—and named it the Blue Dolphin. Gene helped me learn to drive. Relishing freedom and independence, I explored options for furthering my education after high school. When the mailbox filled up with college catalogs, Mom took me aside in the kitchen, the talking room.

"Honey, we want you to go to college, but you'll have to do it on your own. We don't have the money."

"I know. I'm just exploring what's possible. I'm still saving up."

"We'd help, it's just that, well…"

"What's going on, Mom? You look tired. Are you and Gene doing okay?"

Her sudden smile surprised me. "Better than ever, Jerry, and I can finally answer the question you asked before I married your stepdad."

"You mean, 'Do you love him?' That question?"

"Yes, that one. We may have married each other out of need, but I do love him, and he loves me. He wanted Greg to have a family, and I wanted him for you boys and me. And now, we're in love. Definitely."

"I already knew that. My bedroom's right next to yours, and I've heard you guys a few times."

She blushed and looked down. "Stop that. You did not!" Then she looked up again, like a timid little girl. "Really, you heard us?"

"The walls are thin. I'm glad you're happy."

The next morning, after serving French toast and bacon to the family at breakfast, Mom and Gene stood at the head of the table with their arms around each other, and Mom made an announcement.

"Boys, your dad and I have something to share."

"Are you pregnant?" Bob asked.

"How'd you know?"

"You two have been whispering together for a week. I thought you might be."

"When are you due, Mom?" I asked.

"In five or six months."

"Boy or girl?" Roger asked.

"We don't know," Gene explained, "but we're hoping for a girl. Right, Ellie?"

"A girl would be lovely."

"Or a boy," Greg chimed in. "I hope it's a boy."

"Me too," Roger added. "I want a boy."

Exasperated and happy, Mom said, "Oh, you kids. Your lunches are ready. Brush your teeth and get to school."

Mom got her wish. Angelic and healthy, Lori came into our world six months later.

By this time, my close friends had cars. Taking advantage of our independence, Duane and I and two others piled into one car on a Saturday night and drove to Boulder, twenty-six miles away. The legal age for drinking 3.2% beer in Colorado was eighteen. We'd heard of a western-themed bar that didn't look too closely at IDs. We passed the checkpoint, entered the dank, cavernous interior, took a table in the back, listened to the latest country hits, told each other tall tales, and sipped beer after beer. After beer after beer.

Around midnight the bouncer escorted us to our car. Before he'd let us get in it, he asked, "Which one of you boys is fit to drive?"

"Not me, that's for certain." I laughed a little too loudly. For the first time in my life, I was absolutely hammered—three, four, or five sheets to the wind.

My friends, less wasted than I, stuffed my body into the backseat, and we made to Chase Street without incident. Duane dragged me out of the car and deposited me the front step. "You're on your own from here, buddy. Good luck."

I don't remember going inside, getting into my bedroom, or crawling under the covers, but I vividly recall what happened the next morning.

Mom knocked on my door and walked in at ten a.m. She pulled up the window shade, flooding the room with sunlight. I moaned and covered my eyes with my hands.

"Are you finally awake, honey?"

I hadn't looked up yet, but I could tell she stood over the bed with her arms folded over her chest.

"Yeah, barely," I grunted. "God, what's that smell?"

"Vomit, dear. Your waste can is half-full. Does your stomach hurt?"

"Uhhh. So bad." The tapping of her foot sounded intimidating.

"What about your head?"

"It's pounding."

"Good!" she said, her voice a notch higher. "Don't you ever come home drunk again. Not in my house, ever! Now get out of bed, clean up your mess, shower and get dressed. Only then will I give you some aspirin." She slammed the door on her way out.

That was the first and last time I've ever gotten that smashed on alcohol.

Brother Bob graduated from high school, found work in construction, married his childhood sweetheart, and moved out of the house. I left home the following year and enrolled at Adam's State College in Alamosa, Colorado.

Two years later, I visited Chase Street for a weekend visit with the family. The appetizer for supper was another announcement from Mom and Gene. They stood at the head of the table with their arms around each other.

Mom spoke first. "We have something to tell you."

"You're pregnant again," I blurted out.

Gene's proud grin shifted to one of surprise. "How'd you know?"

"You told us about Lori the exact same way," Roger added.

"Boy or girl?" Greg asked.

"Either one," Mom said, raising both palms. "As long as he or she is healthy."

"Are you guys gonna to kiss or what?" I prodded.

They looked into each other's eyes and smooched.

Beautiful (and healthy) baby Gary arrived seven months later.

As we learned to say in our family, "Life is hard, and it's worth it." Mom and Gene moved into a new, larger house in 1965 with their two youngest kids, Lori and Gary. Working diligently, Gene advanced in his profession and became the first person to be inducted into the World Wide Pet Supply Association Hall of Fame in 2014. They both volunteered with the Westernaires, a Colorado organization that teaches young people to believe in themselves by working with and riding horses. During their fifty-one years together, they square danced, bowled, and traveled internationally, and remained devoted to each other and their six children until the end of their long lives. It took me a few years of experiencing Gene's strong heart before I could shed the title "stepdad," but he finally became "Dad" from the bottom of mine.

Many families rejected their gay children in the 1970s. I asked myself if I could survive the loss of my family's love by telling my parents, even if it broke their hearts. I'd already come out to a psychiatrist in Boulder and had spent months in Mexico with my gay friends.

After accepting the offer to teach at the University of Washington and preparing for the three-day drive from Denver to Seattle, Mom and Gene invited me to lunch prior to the trip. I needed to get out the truth and get them out of the closet with me. Mom felt something was up when I arrived.

"What's the matter, honey? Are you worried about the long drive to Seattle?"

"No, Mom. I have something to tell you and Dad."

"Are you okay, Son?" asked Dad.

"I'm okay, but let's go outside in the backyard. I need the sun today."

Mom filled our glasses with iced tea as we sat at the picnic table under the eaves. With shoulders slumped, I took a full breath, raised my head, and looked across the table at my parents waiting patiently with a tinge of suspense.

"This may come as a surprise, and I don't mean to upset you, but you need to know… you deserve to know." I paused and took another deep breath. "I'm different than most guys. I'm homosexual."

Time paused and took a deeper breath as the words sunk in.

"No, you're not!" Mom's eyebrows shot up as her chin tucked backwards. "You're normal. You're my Jerry."

"Yes, I'm your Jerry, and I'm normal, and I'm homosexual."

"Who molested you?" she cried. "Tell me! Who did it?"

"I wasn't molested, Mom." I sighed and shook my

head a little. "It's just who I am."

"Are you certain?" Dad asked. "I mean, could it just be a phase? Something you can get through?"

"No, Dad, I'm certain. I've known for a while now. I can't change."

Mom began to cry. Standing up, she bumped the table and spilled her tea. "I won't have it, Jerry. You cannot be homosexual. You can't."

"I'm sorry Mom."

She headed toward the house, weeping while she walked.

As I watched her disappear through the door, my eyes brimmed with tears.

Dad reached across the table and held my hand. "Son, I understand. I've traveled further in the world than has your mother. I met a few homosexuals in the military, and they were good guys. You're a good guy, Jerry. If this is who you are, know that we love you. We always will, no matter what."

I took a quick breath and relaxed my shoulders a bit. "Thanks for your support, but I'm worried about Mom."

"Well… this has been quite a shock for her." Dad thought for a moment and glanced over at the house, up to the bedroom where she'd probably gone. "Give her some time. She'll come around. I know she will."

I left home feeling better and worse, bittersweet, with two emotions conversing in my chest—one lung sighing with relief, the other answering with a sigh of sadness. My heart floundered in between. I arrived in Seattle on schedule, met my colleagues, found an apartment, and had my phone installed. I called home, and Mom answered.

"Oh, Jerry, I'm so glad it's you. I want to tell you something. It's very important."

"Okay, Mom." I was nervous but felt the love coursing in her voice.

"I've had time to think about you, and about what you told us. I watch the *Phil Donahue Show* every afternoon, you know. And he's been interviewing homosexuals... and well... they're normal like you! I'm so sorry."

We both dissolved in tears.

"I love you, Jerry," she sobbed. "I love you."

"I love you too, Mom. We're family, and that's what matters."

As I write these words decades later, my five splendid siblings—Bob, Roger, Greg, Lori and Gary—have all married, had children, and led happy, productive lives. Most of them are relatively healthy and retired. We owe much of our success to Gene and his strong heart.

This courageous gentleman entered our lives in 1957 and became a role model for compassion, friendship, acceptance and kindness. He truly was a blessing. I can still hear Mom saying, "God answered my prayers."

And I can still hear brother Bob's words at Gene's funeral, simple yet right to the core. "Dad played a very important role in all of our lives. He showed me how to love a woman." He paused and pointed to his wife JoAnn in the sanctuary filled with folks who'd come to honor Gene. "This is why we have been happily married for more than fifty years."

~ ~ ~

# Reservoirs of Courage

*Fear and Courage are Brothers.*
~Proverb~

## Sri Lanka, 2001

POINTING A SEMI-AUTOMATIC ASSAULT RIFLE at the center of my chest, a young soldier stepped from behind the sandbag bunker.

"Stop! Hands up! Papers!"

As he shouted, another soldier appeared from somewhere and covered my back. I slowly reached into my front pocket and produced a copy of my passport. The first soldier checked to see if the photo matched my face and then patted me down from shoulders to ankles. To make sure I wasn't hiding a hand grenade in my underwear, the soldier behind me reached up and squeezed my testicles.

"Christ!" I yelled.

Both men laughed, and the tension eased. I managed a meek smile.

"You want to walk there?" asked the lead soldier as he gestured down the street with his rifle.

"Yes, please."

He blew his whistle loud enough to cause the guards a block away to look over their bunker. He pointed me out, and they understood. I was good to go at least another block.

One week earlier, one corner away from where I stood, twelve people died when a bus blew up on this busy boulevard a few steps from the famous Galle Face Hotel in the capital city of Columbo, Sri Lanka.

I blame this harrowing experience in a war-torn country on Marco Polo. A voracious reader from childhood, I had discovered a dog-eared paperback entitled *The Travels of Marco Polo* on the highest shelf of my junior high school library. Born into a Venetian merchant family in the mid-13th century, Marco left home as a teenager and traveled with his father and uncle throughout China, India and beyond. They were intent on opening Asia's Silk Road, and young Marco kept a diary of his adventures covering a span of twenty-four years. Inspired by the stories, I became enamored with his descriptions of Ceylon, renamed Sri Lanka in 1972. Marco wrote about wild cinnamon growing in abundance on the island and about the Sinhalese people who had skin the color of gold. In all his journeys, he'd never seen a more beautiful land and seascape. I pledged at age fifteen that one day I'd travel halfway around the world to explore this island nation and meet the golden-hued inhabitants.

Forty-three years later in 2001, I accepted an invitation to join an around-the-world cruise as guest storyteller and author. I flew from the United States to Darwin, Australia, embarked on the ship, and sailed to East Timor, on towards Indonesia with brief stops in Flores, Bali, and Singapore, and finally arrived in Colombo. My two weeks aboard ship was over, but I stayed to explore the safer parts of Sri Lanka for seven more days.

Eighteen years after the civil war had begun in 1983, the country of Sri Lanka was still a perilous place to visit. The Tamil Tigers' insurgency against the government in order to create an independent state wreaked havoc throughout the island. Over-populated, ecologically devastated, and war-torn, Sri Lanka had lost much of its beauty. Its infrastructure was unstable and travel difficult as well as dangerous.

However, the people were truly gorgeous, both the native Sinhalese, and the darker-skinned Tamil who, hundreds of years earlier, had been brought from the Southern tip of India to work the land. I'll never forget the moments I watched a stately, slender, golden Sinhalese woman glide through the hotel lobby. A super being, I thought, with inborn nobility.

After three days in Colombo, I hired a taxi and headed to Negombo, a small coastal town 37 kilometers north. It was an arduous, two-hour trek on a potholed highway crowded with diesel-spewing trucks, plodding water buffalo pulling heavy carts, and overburdened motorbikes carrying entire families and their groceries. A crumbling concrete bridge spanning the reeking sewer of a river shook as we crossed. Trembling, I uttered a brief prayer to my guardian angels.

Upon arriving, I checked in and ventured out to explore the area. My beach hotel was breathtaking in all the wrong ways. I unfolded my blanket on filthy sand littered with plastic trash that exuded an overpowering stench of decaying fish. I trudged to the next beach over and discovered more dead fish. The thousands of tiny silver fish netted that morning had been spread out on the sand to dry and were not the golden beach companions I'd imagined. The sun warmed, the sea invited, but the water looked unclean and unsafe. Overtaken by weariness, I found my way back to my blanket and collapsed.

I didn't hear his approach until he spoke. His command of English was precise and enticing.

"Mister! Excuse me, mister, can I talk with you?"

I opened my eyes and saw a Sinhalese youth hovering over me.

"You want to talk?"

I sat up and blinked several times, trying to focus. I guessed he was about age 17. The boy was tall, athletic, and wore a Speedo swimsuit. His bronze skin shimmered in the afternoon light as he looked skyward and shook his head, sweeping the mane of thick, black hair across his strong shoulders.

He looked back down at me with intelligent eyes. "You don't look Dutch. Are you British?"

"I'm an American."

"I've never met an American!" Uninvited, he sat on the corner of my blanket and folded his long legs into a half-lotus position. "Yes, let's talk. My name is Nehan. And you are?"

"I'm Pleasant. Nice to meet you." I was mesmerized but squeezed out a smile. "Yes, let's talk."

"The British and Dutch colonized my poor country a long time ago. That's why they come back."

"Your English is quite good, Nehan."

"I know," he proudly announced. "I study hard. I'll work for a tourist company in one more year. I must help my family to live better."

"Tell me about your family."

"We live down the beach. Mama, Papa, Grandmother, my younger sister and me."

"You have a house?"

"A small house. Three rooms and a bathroom. We wash clothes in the yard."

"What does your father do?"

"Papa can't work. He's blind. Mama rents beach chairs and sells coconuts to thirsty people. Now you tell me about you. What is your job? Where in America do you live? Tell me the names of your children. How many cars do you have?"

I chuckled. "That's a lot of questions! Well... I'm a

single man. I never married. I have no children. I've got one old car. I've made a career as a storyteller, finding and shaping tales to write and share. I live in Albany, New York on the east coast of the United States, but I've traveled far in the world. Not everywhere though, and this is my first time in Sri Lanka. Like you, I am interested in people."

We traded questions and answers for an hour that zipped by. As the sun was about to drop into the ocean, I asked one last question. "What is your dream for the future, Nehan?"

He sighed. "I want to see the world... like you."

"That's a wonderful dream that I'm still working on." I stood and put on my shirt. Nehan stood as well, and facing me, did something unexpected. He pantomimed removing his eyes and gently placing them in my shirt pocket.

"Take my eyes with you, Mr. Pleasant." He spoke with hope and reverence. "Show me the world."

I shook the hand of this princely youth and nodded. "I will, my friend. I will."

Though he may not have known consciously, at a deeper level of awareness he seemed to understand the archetypical story, myth, or legend found in most cultures about the necessity of losing your eyes in order to see. I met and befriended other fascinating people during my brief week in Sri Lanka, but Nehan is who I reflect upon most often.

## Seattle, Washington, 1984

Being gay in America during the 1980s was a time of despair, a time of uncertainty, a time of loss. Day to day, I lived in fear of the virus that was devastating the lives of my gay brothers. President Ronald Reagan refused to publicly say the word AIDS until 1986, the sixth year of the epidemic. Reverend Jerry Falwell spewed inflammatory opinions from his pulpit that AIDS was God's punishment for homosexuals and God's punishment for a society that even tolerates homosexuals. If my gay brothers didn't succumb to the virus, they faced the possibility of death at the righteous hands of those who believed they should never have been born. I met Jason during the summer after a swim at the University of Washington's intermural building. I showered, wrapped a towel around my waist, and entered the men's sauna. Only one guy sat on the top of the three-tiered bench in the cedar-paneled room. Under bushy light brown hair, his pock-marked face was drenched in sweat.

He greeted me with a strained smile and a "Hey."

"Hey back," I said. "It's pretty quiet today."

"Yeah. Summertime. Most of the other students are gone."

I sat on the lower tier, and the young lad moved down one row.

A few moments later, he asked, "Can I talk to you about something?"

"Sure. What's up?" At age 41, I didn't think he was coming on to me, nor was I interested in a date with the stranger.

"I just got some bad news."

"Well that doesn't sound good."

He began to cry. "Sorry, I'm sorry," he managed to whisper amidst the tears flowing from his bright blue eyes. "It's just that I can't tell anyone."

"It's all right. We don't even know each other, but I'm here. Now. Tell *me*."

He paused and sweated, inside and out. "I went back to the clinic this morning... They gave me the results of the tests. I have AIDS... And I'm scared."

"That is scary." I asked his name and let him talk.

"My name's Jason. I'm gay. I'm a music student in my second year and work part-time job at the University Book Store. I share an apartment with a friend. Things seemed to be going well, but I started losing weight, slowly, for weeks."

I sat quietly, listening intently with my chin resting on my hands, looking at our feet. His feet were big, and I wondered what size they were. I thought of my brother. Roger's feet are size fourteen.

"Then this constant fatigue kicked in, and I couldn't shake a nasty cough." He paused again, then sighed, "I'm going to die, I guess."

Dripping wet from the intense heat and these honest words pounding in my chest, I said, "Okay, I've lost enough weight for today. C'mon, let's shower and get dressed. I'll meet you on the front steps. We can talk further."

We found a secluded spot under a shade tree near the entrance of the intermural building and sat on the grass.

"Pleasant... why are you so kind?"

"I'm gay, too, and I've already lost two friends. I know how hard this can be. You have friends, right?"

"Yes, but I can't tell them. I can't."

"You'll need support, Jason."

"But what if they reject me?"

"Your friends, if they are true friends, won't reject you. What about your parents?"

"I can't talk to them either. They hate that I'm gay. Especially my dad. He said I'm going to hell and won't even talk to me anymore."

"That's rough. Do they have religious issues?"

"It's more about the military than religion. He's a

retired army colonel. And he's ashamed of me."

"How about your mother?"

"She's a military wife. She does what he says. He's in charge."

"Does your mother love you?"

"I suppose. But now? Who knows?"

I let the conversation sit for a minute and wandered through my heart. I wanted to help him and knew I could, but how? "Are you dating anyone? Is there a boyfriend in the picture?"

"He dumped me last month. He couldn't stand that I'm tired all the time. I don't go out anymore. No more drinking and dancing. I hate it. He hates it."

"Your roommate?"

"He's gay and a good friend. We get on pretty well."

"How many real friends do you have in Seattle?"

He thought for a moment and said, "Three, including my roommate."

"Did the doctor give you a list of support groups when you got the diagnosis this morning?"

"Yes, but—"

"No buts," I said. "You need help, and I know of two great groups that helped my friends. The Seattle Gay Clinic and the Chicken Soup Brigade. Check in with them. You don't have to do this alone."

"I don't want to die, Pleasant. I'm too young!"

"Yes, you are young. Too young. So, keep living. As long as you can."

Jason's apartment was on Capitol Hill, not far from mine. He told his friends and family he was sick. I visited when I could, bearing raspberry smoothies and chocolate donuts. During the next six months, his health continued to decline. He quit his job and dropped out of school. Soon after, he moved back home with his parents.

I called Jason to ask if I could visit, and he gave me the address of his childhood home. I arrived late one Saturday morning, walked the brick path up to a stately home, and rang the bell.

The retired army colonel answered the door. Tall and fit, wearing trousers creased and grey hair trimmed short, he looked me over, his eyes intense. "Yes?"

"Hello, sir. I'm Jason's friend. I'd like to visit with him and see how he's doing."

The colonel responded with a wicked whisper. "Leave. None of Jason's friends are welcome here." He shoved the door closed, and I heard the click of the lock.

I called Jason when I got home. "Hey, buddy, what's going on? I stopped by to visit you and met your father. He shut the door in my face."

"Doesn't surprise me. He hardly talks to me. Thanks for trying."

"No problem. How're you doin'?"

"Not so hot," he admitted. "I have rashes, night sweats, and shingles. I look as bad as I feel. Dad can't stand me."

"Your mother?"

"She cries a lot, but she's caring for me."

I had a sudden thought, or maybe *heard* a voice of hope. My higher self, perhaps? An image appeared of Jason and his dad having a real conversation like my father and I. "Ask your dad to tell you some of his stories, about his childhood, the end of WWII, his battles."

"He never talks about the war. It's too personal."

"Tell him that you don't have much time left, and you want to know him better. Ask him to do this for you."

"You think so? I don't know."

"Please do it for me… and for you… and for your dad."

"Okay. I'll try."

After that call I spoke with Jason on the phone every few days. Some were good and others weren't. One day I happened to call on a good one. "How are things going with your dad?"

"Better," Jason said. "He's agreed to tell me one story each day, and I have to tell him one of mine. He wants to know me better, too."

I shouted to myself in silence, "Yes!" I was so happy to hear this.

The following week Jason called me, his breath labored, his voice weak, but strong enough to tell me the latest news. "Dad came close to dying many times at the end of the war. He lost many young men, and he still feels so bad. He even said *I'm* brave now. Isn't that amazing?"

"Yes, that is amazing, and so are you. You are a brave man, Jason. And what about your stories?"

"I told him how alone I felt when I knew I was gay and how afraid I was to come out. I didn't want to disappoint him, you know?"

"I know, I know. I went through the same trials with my family."

"I've told him about my friends, including you, Pleasant, and what good people I've had in my life." His voice grew weaker, until it was barely a whisper. "My liver stopped working yesterday. The doctor said it's nearly over. I'm calling to say goodbye."

My heart dropped into my shoes. "Jason, hang up and hang on, please. I'm coming to see you right now."

I drove too fast and cried during the entire trip but pulled myself together before jumping out of the car. I rushed to the front porch and rang the bell.

Soon the colonel opened the door. Sadness seemed to radiate from his eye, and his voice wavered as he greeted me. "All of Jason's friends are welcome here."

I went inside and said goodbye to my friend.

*Life shrinks or expands*
*in proportion to one's courage.*
~Anais Nin~

Courage marks the path of light and life. You need courage to live and you need courage to die. You need courage to marry and raise children. You need courage to become educated and find passion in your work. You need courage to take care of your body-mind-spirit. You need courage to believe in the Creator and to believe in yourself. Fill your reservoir of courage with kindness, selflessness, humility, integrity, and patience.

**Kindness**

I often tip the vegetable lady who buys produce from a wholesale market in the morning and sets up a table in the afternoon across from my condo in Chiang Mai. Because she doesn't pay rent to use the sidewalk, she prices her goods accordingly. Tipping in Thailand is not common and often unexpected, especially for vendors on the streets. Give someone a tiny tip over the "correct" amount, and they'll try hard to give it back to you.

One day I filled a bag with ripe tomatoes, onions, red and yellow bell peppers, garlic and lettuce, all for sixty baht or $1.80, and handed the vegetable lady three twenty-baht bills. Then I reached into my pocket and gave her another five-baht coin. (That's only fifteen cents!)

Her eyes and smile widened. "Thank you, thank you."

I mirrored her smile. "You are so welcome."

"Why you do this?"

"You work so hard, and your smile is beautiful."

I like the feeling of my heart expanding. Kindness creates happiness, and we can never have too much happiness.

## Selflessness

A simple definition of selflessness: Be more concerned with the needs and desires of others that with your own. This definition considers the need to take care of yourself in order to help take care of others. Giving can ease the suffering of others, but if you suffer in order to give, so does your heart.

My step-dad took on a huge task by marrying my mother. His selflessness showed through time and again. He took care of himself by stretching, exercising, eating right, and laughing loud when he was happy. In his later years, he'd enjoy a big bowl of freshly popped, salted and buttered popcorn every night after dinner. When visitors dropped in, as they often did, he'd offer them one handful. If they accepted, he'd say with a grin, "This bowl is mine, but let me make one for you."

## Humility

Most of us are not born into wealth and fame. Our humble origins create the desire for success earned rather than given. My heroes, in stories and real-life, display humility as a second skin, natural rather than forced. Arrogance, egoism, and self-importance often lead to family dramas with unfortunate outcomes. Conversely, humility sets the stage for your human dramas to play out into genuinely happy endings. Brother

Jaguar and Jason's dad shared the power of humility with Gene, though it took them a while to realize it. Where does humility play its role in your life?

## Integrity

Being true to yourself and others requires courage. There is only one you, and your thoughts and words must align with *your* actions. The Latin word 'integer' means whole and complete. Regardless of the circumstances, the real, authentic you evolves through consistency in your actions. As Henry Ward Beecher said, "A man is rich or poor according to what he is, not according to what he has."

## Patience

Several times over the course of my storytelling career, I've been mistakenly introduced as "Patience" De-Spain, a name I've always appreciated. For much of my life, I've held close the words inscribed on a motivational poster by the British as they prepared for World War II.

*Keep calm and carry on.*

Patience may be the key to your success in life and enlightenment. Life isn't perfect. If you expect the world to always run smoothly, you'll likely create impatience, frustration, and stress—for you and for others around you. Remaining calm in traffic jams or while waiting in long lines to pay for groceries is not only a virtue but a sign of genuine strength. The gift of patience keeps your reservoirs of courage full.

~ ~ ~

# Soul

## CHAPTER EIGHT

*Love is
the beauty
of the soul.*

~Saint Augustine~

# Old Joe and the Carpenter

## United States

OLD JOE, A FARMER WITH DIRT under his fingernails, loved the seed, soil, sun, and rain. During the good years, his crops were bountiful, and during the hard years, they held their own and delivered. His land in Kentucky had been in his family for generations, but now he was alone and getting older. Martha, his beloved wife of forty-seven years, had recently passed. Their only child lived far away in Colorado with her husband, sons, and daughters.

He wasn't entirely alone. His best friend, Captain Beauregard Floyd, lived on the farm right next to him and was nearly Old Joe's age. Everyone called him Beau, and his red barn sat within sight of Old Joe's front porch. They looked in on each other about once a week to share a drink, a story, and if times weren't too tough, a few belly laughs.

One Saturday morning, Joe argued with his neighbor over a stray heifer on Beau's land. "That there heifer's mine, ya know."

Beau disagreed. "Nope. She's mine."

Old Joe shook his head in disgust. "Y'all are blind in

one eye and can't see outta the other. She got the same color as my Guernsey and the same white markings."

Like two bulls snorting and stomping the ground in a face-off, the stubborn old grumps refused to back down.

"Wait a cotton-pickin' minute now. You are gettin' on my last nerve. That darn heifer is mine, I say."

"By God, she's mine, and that's that," Beau raged.

Old Joe saw Beau's rage and raised it another notch. "I tell you what… then keep her, you old fart, and don't ever bother me again."

"Count on it!" Beau shouted as he jabbed his finger toward Joe's farm. "Now get your butt off my land!"

A miserable month went by without a word between them. Early one morning Joe sat brooding in his oak rocking chair. A knock on the front door interrupted his foul mood. He dragged his stiff body out of the chair, shuffled to the door, and opened it an inch.

A young bearded man tipped his hat and smiled through the crack. "Good day to you, sir."

Joe looked up at his face, then down to the wooden carpenter's box filled with well-worn tools at his feet. "Mornin'. What can I do for you?"

"Well, sir, I'm a travelling carpenter and quite good with my hands. If you have a project or two, anything you'd like some help with, I'm the man for the job."

"Hmm." Old Joe stepped onto the porch. "Wha'd'ya charge for the day?"

"Whatever you decide my work is worth, sir."

"Turns out I might have some work for y'all. Take a gander at that red barn over yonder?"

"Yes, sir. I see it."

"That's my neighbor's, and we got a feud goin' on. And that creek there? It used to be a li'l riv'let runnin' all along our property line."

"What happened?"

"He took his dadburn tractor and plowed that skinny furrow wide and flooded it from his upper pond. Now we got this deep creek between us. Lately I been chewin' on a thought, and I want to do him one better."

"How's that?" asked the carpenter.

"I don't want to see his place no more, dagnabbit. I got a barn full of boards, nails, sawhorses, and whatever y'all need to build me a tall fence on my side of the line. That'll teach him."

The young man nodded. "I won't disappoint you, sir. We'll teach him a lesson!"

"I'm fixin' to head into town for some grub and supplies, and reckon I'll be back 'round sunset. Get as much work done as you can."

"I will do my best."

Old Joe hitched his strongest horse to the wagon, yanked the reigns, and disappeared over the hill.

The young carpenter carried lumber and sawhorses to the edge of the creek and began his project. He worked hard, took few breaks, measured, sawed, and hammered with skill and determination. He finished as the sun began to set, and Old Joe pulled into the farmyard.

After Old Joe whispered, "What in tarnation?", he sat speechless in his wagon, his mouth open gathering flies. Instead of a tall fence, a stately footbridge with handrails spanned the creek from one side to the other. As Old Joe climbed down from the wagon, he saw Beau walking across the bridge with his hands outstretched.

When Beau reached Old Joe, he grabbed his hand in a vice grip. "You old coot, you! I am glad you did this. I don't need that dern calf." Beau pulled Old Joe into a bear hug. "I just want us to be friends like before."

"I don't want that heifer, neither. Friends we are, as always." With his arm still around Beau, Old Joe pointed over at the carpenter. "This here bridge was that fella's idea, and I am glad he built it."

The carpenter had packed up his tools and started to leave.

"Hold yer horses, young man!" Old Joe tramped over to him and stuffed a wad of bills into his shirt pocket. "Beau and I know ev'rybody in this whole valley. We could help you keep busier than popcorn in a hot fryin' pan."

"Thanks for the cash and your offer. I'd like to stay, but I can't. I've got more bridges to build."

~ ~ ~

# Life Goes On

*There is only one happiness in this life,*
*to love and be loved.*
~George Sand~

WHEN I WAS NINE YEARS OLD, I remember walking home from school on a Tuesday afternoon and pondering my future. I found Mom washing vegetables for dinner in the kitchen on Chase Street.

"Honey, you look so serious. What's going on?"

"Mom… I've made some decisions."

"About what?"

"My life."

"That's good. What've you decided?"

"One, I don't want to be in the army this time."

"I'm glad, Jerry. I don't want you to, either. No mother does. What else?"

"Two, I'm not going to have a regular job this time."

"You're a smart boy. You'll get a good education and have a fine job."

"I know mom. Just not a regular job. I want more than that."

"Okay. Have you decided anything else?"

"Yes. Three, I'm not getting married this time."

Mom dried her hands on the dish towel and hugged me. "Oh, honey, you'll fall in love and get married. You'll be a wonderful husband and father. Now change your clothes and go outside to play. I've got a lot of work to do."

I'd forgotten this scene entirely until 31 years later when I was 40, at home with the family in Colorado for Christmas and helping Mom in the kitchen.

"Pleasant," she asked, "do you remember what you told me about the decisions you'd made when you were in what... the third grade?"

Visions of the scene flashed in my mind. "Yes, I remember. And all three came true. I wasn't drafted in the Vietnam War. I don't have a 'normal' kind of job, and I'm not married."

"I've wondered how you knew that such a young age. And what did you mean by 'this time'?

"This life."

"This life? I still don't understand."

I gave Mom a hug and shared the truth I'd learned after years of meditating and searching. "I believe that we live many physical lives here on Earth, and in this one, I'm blessed to have you as my mother and Gene as my stepdad."

"What about love? Your dad and I have talked about it. We want you to find and love a good man. You can be married in the eyes of God."

I found love four months later in the spring of 1983. The avocado-green phone on the kitchen wall of my small San Diego apartment rang. My good friend, meditator, and gym aficionado Douglas asked, "Wanna go to a party tonight?"

"What kind of party?"

"My friend Sara's hosting an open house for meditators of the transcendental type, like us. Wine, cheese and crackers, conversation, that sort of thing."

"Not too exciting, I guess"

"Probably not, but we can sneak out for dinner after making an appearance."

"Okay," I agreed. "Let's do it."

"I'll pick you up at seven."

I liked going out with Douglas, a successful attorney who didn't take himself too seriously and could completely relax in social outings. He enjoyed the role of wingman and helped me meet interesting guys at San Diego's restaurants and bars.

Sara's gathering turned out to be quite lively and packed with rooms full of meditators, multi-generational, multi-colored, straight and gay. A Baroque flute bridging heaven and earth played in the background. Hints of soft creamy sandalwood tickled my nose. Red wine and rich conversations flowed throughout her home.

Douglas and I lost each other in the mix. After sitting for an hour in the crowded living room while talking with delightful strangers, hunger kicked in. I excused myself and searched for Douglas.

A guy bumped into me in the dining room and

apologized, "Sorry, man."

"Totally okay," I said, raising one hand and both eyebrows. 'Totally okay' had been an understatement. He was a quantum leap beyond okay, and I stood soaking in his young, beautiful, six-foot-tall, V-shaped, muscular body. His white shirt with the top two buttons undone emphasized his hairless, well-defined chest. Tight denim jeans, bright blue eyes, bushy blonde hair with streaks of gold, and a shy smile completed the look. I held out my hand. "Pleasant."

He looked confused. "It is… a pleasant party."

"Yes, it is, and Pleasant is my first name. A family tradition from way back."

He shook my hand. "What a cool name. I'm Ryder, with a y."

"I like it. Are you a meditator?"

"Yeah, since I was seventeen, so about eight years. I just graduated from Maharishi International University in Fairfield, Iowa. Do you know it?"

"Quite well. I've visited twice for month-long courses. Wish I'd seen you there."

Ryder gestured around the room. "You know many of these people?"

"Not really, I haven't been in San Diego that long."

"I just got here last week, and—"

Douglas sidled up to me. "Here you are. Ready for dinner? And who's this? Introduce me right now."

"Douglas, Ryder. Ryder, Douglas."

"Great name, buddy. Would you like to have dinner with us? My treat."

"Thanks a lot for the offer, but I've already eaten. A strict vegetarian and all that. And I just arrived at these parts, so maybe a rain check?"

"Of course," Douglas said. "You got his number?"

"Actually, no. We just met." I took a card from my

wallet and handed it to Ryder. "Here's my name and number. Give me a call. I'd like to get to know you better."

"Thanks! Nice to meet you. You too, Douglas."

Douglas and I headed to a popular Mexican place, sat at one of the eight wooden tables covered with red-and-white checkered plastic, and ordered a platter of chips and guacamole, margaritas, and two of their excellent fish tacos.

"Ryder." Douglas spoke as if it were on a marque in Hollywood. "What a name and what a look! He could be a model. How old is he?"

"Twenty-five is what he implied."

"Gay?"

"No idea."

"But you'd like to date him?"

"Well, yeah. He's a serious meditator, fresh from college, beautiful, built, and yeah again, I'd love to date him."

"He's what, fifteen years younger than you?"

"Yup. But Douglas, let's be honest here. He's far beyond my reach."

"Oh, no! Not the 'I'm not worthy' speech. I've heard this before. Give yourself a break."

"What are the odds that he'll actually call me?"

"He gave you a major smile when you gave him your card. I bet he'll call." Douglas lifted his margarita glass and clicked mine. "Cheers to Ryder and the future!"

I shrugged my shoulders and toasted.

After dinner, Douglas wasn't done. "Wanna go dancing? Lots of sailors are in town. The Brass Rail will be jumping."

"Sure, but only for an hour. I'm working on a new collection of multicultural tales and have to get up early tomorrow."

"How early?"

"Nine."

"Good. We're going dancing!"

The night was fun, but I couldn't let go of Ryder's image, even while dancing to the heavy rock beats with horny regulars and visiting sailors. I went home happy and exhausted. As I crawled into bed alone, I felt Ryder's strong, friendly grip on my hand and my heart.

He didn't call. Not the next day. Not the next week. I was disappointed, but not surprised. Too young, I thought. Too beautiful. A dream too big. Get over it, Pleasant.

Another week went by. Each time the phone rang, I felt renewed hope, but began to forget about Ryder.

On a Wednesday afternoon of the third week, he called. "Uh, hi, Pleasant. This is Ryder, from the meditator's party? You remember?"

My heart skipped a beat. A cliché maybe, but I actually felt a thump in my chest and had to take a fresh breath. "Hi, Ryder. Of course, I remember you! I'm happy to hear from you."

"I lost your card that night, too many people and all. But I've been thinking about you and storytelling. I went back to Sara's house and asked if she knew you and the other guy, Douglas. She gave me his number, and he gave me yours. I hope that's okay."

"Perfectly okay. What's up?"

"I'd like to meet and talk. You sounded really interesting, and I don't have many friends here yet."

Crossing my fingers, I asked, "How about coming over for dinner tomorrow night? I'll make a vegetarian meal for us."

"Sure, but I'm eating fish again. And eggs. Lots of changes now that I'm back in society. You know how restricted life is at MIU."

"I understand completely. Does seven p.m. work for you?"

"Sounds great. I'll bring some beer."

I gave Ryder my address, hung up, and stood motionless—except for my quivering hands and pulsing heart.

Douglas called later in the day. "Did you hear from Ryder?"

"I did. And he's coming over for dinner tomorrow."

"Cool. Can I join you?"

"Absolutely... not!"

"Just kidding. God, he sounds so sweet on the phone. Don't let him get away. And do everything I'd do."

"I'm not likely to attack him on the first date, bud."

"Okay, but I bet you'll think about it. Have a good time, and I'll want all the details the morning after."

The next day, I cleaned, shopped, showered, and prepared our meal—asparagus spears packed in foil, topped with a fillet of salmon, butter, and lemon slices, ready to pop into the oven, and a wilted spinach salad with eggs and green onions. Soon after seven the doorbell buzzed. I took a deep breath and opened the door.

Ryder stood on the steps with his six-pack stomach and a six-pack of Budweiser in hand. "I didn't know what kind of beer—"

"Bud's perfect for buds. C'mon in."

"Nice place you got here." Ryder checked out my small, sparsely furnished apartment while I checked out Ryder. "Mind if I see the bathroom next? I gotta pee."

"Door on the right."

I stared at his tight butt as he glided away. For his size and obvious strength, his movements were filled with an inborn grace. I listened intently to the flush of the toilet and the rush of the sink faucet until Ryder walked back into the living room.

"Bathrooms say a lot about a guy. You live clean, Pleasant. I like that."

"My mother's influence. I like order. It makes sense to me."

"Me, too."

I handed him a cold beer. "Have a seat on the sofa, if you like. We can talk while I put dinner in the oven."

"Tell me about storytelling."

I gave him a ten-minute rundown of the last few years. "Now it's your turn. Tell me about life at Maharishi International University, and what you're up to now."

Ryder grinned. "I'll need another beer for that."

Once accommodated, he launched into his tale. "I fell in love with meditation the first time I tried it. I wanted an education and enlightenment, so I enrolled after high school. After four-and-a-half years, I graduated with a bachelor's degree in environmental science, and moved from the corn fields, pig farms, and dreary winter of Iowa to sunny San Diego two months ago."

"Do you have a job now?"

"I'm driving a cab to make enough to live on. My degree hasn't panned out yet. And I'm still adjusting to the real world, you know?"

I knew exactly how Ryder felt. "You mean where everyone isn't always smiling, speaking quietly, and meditating twice each day?"

"More like four times a day. I loved it, and studying was easy. I made good grades."

"How'd you get in such great shape? You play sports at MIU?"

"No, but I ran regularly and worked out using my

body weight. You know, push-ups, pull-ups, sit-ups, and stuff like that."

"How about relationships? Did you fall in love with anyone?"

"God, no. Men are kept separate from women nearly all the time. Separate dorms, separate meditation halls, even separate dining halls. We were there to evolve as fast as possible."

"So not much sex?"

"No sex for me. I lost interest after the first few months."

"And now that you're free?"

Ryder shifted in his seat and looked at me nervously. "Our dinner smells good. Time to eat?"

The table was set. I pulled the salmon and asparagus from the oven, filled our plates, and completed the offering with the spinach salads.

"This looks great! Where'd you learn to cook?"

"In Seattle. I worked in a small French restaurant for a year while trying to make a living as a storyteller."

Ryder took a forkful of salmon and savored it with a grin. "Mmm. Tastes as good as it looks. I'll bet your girlfriends like that you can cook."

"I don't have girlfriends. I'm gay."

Simultaneously shocked and mystified, he stared at me from across the table with his wide-open baby blues. "You're gay? Really?"

"Really."

"But you're happy... I think you're happy. You *seem* happy. How can you be gay *and* happy?"

Genuinely surprised at his naivete, I smiled. "You've lived in a protected environment for a long time, my friend. I've pursued happiness for years. Meditation, great friends, loving myself, and being who I am helps."

"This is amazing. I mean, *you're* amazing. You're the

first gay person I've met. I had no idea you could do this."

"Do what?"

"Be gay and live a good life."

We talked throughout the meal, then continued in the living room until we'd finished the six-pack of beer. It was getting late, and I explained that I needed to go to bed.

"Can we meet again, Pleasant? I don't work on Sundays. We could go to the beach. Do you swim?"

"I do."

"Let's swim and then have lunch on the beach. Wha'd'ya say?"

"I say yes. That would be grand."

After putting on his jacket, Ryder gave me a tentative hug at the door. "See you sooner than later. Two days."

On Sunday Ryder and I changed into our swimsuits in the public locker room at Mission Beach. He stripped off quickly, naturally, revealing the true beauty of his body.

He looked me over as well, a man fifteen years his senior. "You're in good shape. You must swim a lot."

I smiled as I tied my Speedo's drawstring. "I've been at it since I was a kid swimming naked at the Denver YMCA."

"Naked?"

"Right. Swimsuits weren't allowed at the men's Y in the 1950s."

"I love being naked. It feels so much better. Let's take our suits off once we're far enough out, then put them around our necks until we're ready to head into shore."

"You're full of surprises, Ryder."

Our first outing together remains a splendid memory. We swam naked, ate cheeseburgers, drank cokes on the beach, and lay side by side on our towels to talk, snooze, and talk some more.

"Want to be friends, Pleasant?"

"I think we already are. I feel close to you."

He brushed my shoulder with his hand. "Yep, I'd say about six inches close."

We both laughed.

"I feel it, too," Ryder said. "Do you think that's because we both meditate?"

"It's more than that. We're different in many ways, but the differences make no difference... if that makes sense."

"I agree. And I want to share something with you. I mean... Pleasant, I trust you enough to tell you. And all I want is your thoughts on the matter."

"This sounds serious."

We sat up facing each other.

Ryder looked down at his lap. "I can't get an erection. My body won't cooperate, and I don't know what to do."

"When was the last time you ejaculated?"

"When I was nineteen. I had a girlfriend, and we had good sex. Then I went to MIU."

"And?"

"They never came out and said sex was prohibited, but the undercurrent there seemed to say that sex inhibits or slows down enlightenment. After a few months, I lost all interest in it."

"You didn't masturbate in more than four years?"

"True. And now that I'm in the real world, I want sex. But my body... well, it just won't respond"

"Are you aware of the chakras, Ryder?"

"I've heard the term, but that's all."

"The word *chakra* is an old Sanskrit word meaning wheel. Everyone has seven spinning energy centers in our bodies from the base of the spine and to the top of our heads. Breath helps to balance and align them. I believe that your two lower chakras—the Root Chakra and the Sacral Chakra—have shut down. I saw that when I met you. You glow with youth and health from the third chakra up to the seventh. No wonder you can't get hard."

"Should I see a doctor?"

"I don't think you need pills. I've been practicing ancient breath techniques for a few years. Let me show you how to breathe into all your chakras. It might help."

"Here? Now?"

I could see Ryder was ready to try. "No, not in public. Come over the next afternoon you're free. We'll meditate together, and then work on your breathing."

Ryder arrived at my apartment the following Tuesday, full of hope. We chatted for a few moments while I lit a stick of incense, then meditated together on the sofa and shared twenty minutes of silence, peace, and calm.

I arranged a blanket on the floor with a pillow for his head. "You'll lay here, and I'll sit next to you. You can keep your clothes on or take them off, whatever makes you comfortable. You're in a safe space, and I promise you won't be molested."

Ryder laughed as he undressed. "I know you won't hurt me, Pleasant."

He closed his eyes, and I began leading him through the process.

"We'll work on getting your breath all the way down to your Root Chakra. You should feel it at the base of your spine near your tailbone. We'll breathe together.

Follow my slow inhale and even slower exhale."

Ryder's breath relaxed and deepened. After fifteen minutes, he opened his eyes. "I feel something warm down there, like a light... It feels good."

We breathed together for another five minutes.

"Good work, my friend," I said. "Do the breathing each day after your morning meditation, and let nature take her course."

Ryder phoned me two days later. "I got a hard-on! It felt so good!"

"Congratulations. Did you ejaculate?"

He laughed, "I tried, but no cigar. I'm gonna keep working on it, though."

"Sounds great."

"Let's go back to the beach on Sunday. I'll pick you up at eleven."

When Ryder arrived on Sunday, glowing with health and happiness, he jumped out of his car and hugged me hard. "I did it. I ejaculated three times in the last two days. It's amazing. I'm alive again!"

"I'm proud of you, Ryder."

After our swim and lunch on the beach, we shared another serious conversation.

"I don't know how to say this, Pleasant, but I have feelings for you, more than friendship. Feelings in my heart. My heart seems to expand when I'm with you."

"I'm having the same experience being with you. I believe we've been together before, in another life, and here we are in this one, sharing our lives again. I've met a few soul brothers and sisters along the way, but with you, I feel different."

Ryder took my hand and placed it on his bare chest over his beating heart. "I love being with you. That's what I'm trying to say."

"I love us together as well, Ryder. Always have and always will. I'm glad we found each other."

During the next month, we continued sharing meditations, meals, and beach outings. We told stories, laughed, and cried together.

Douglas joined us for dinner out on the town, and afterwards we hung out in our favorite bars. Ryder received lots of attention and danced with guys who didn't try to feel him up. I watched several phone numbers shoved into his shirt pocket. He wasn't vain about his beauty, and after a few beers, he danced along with the rest of us, laughing, sweating, and having the time of his life in a whole new world.

While Douglas and I shared a private luncheon a couple of days later, he said, "Ryder's a gem, Pleasant, even if he isn't gay."

"I think so, too."

Soon the Washington State Arts Commission called. I'd worked with people in the organization for several years, and they asked me to return for my annual school tour. Four weeks, two schools a day, good money. I said yes and asked Ryder to join me.

"Be my road crew. You can help drive and carry my sound equipment. I'll pay for gas, hotels, and meals, and you'll see much of Washington State. You'll meet my friends and some of my family. They will love you."

Ryder thought it over for a moment. "I can quit driving the cab for a month. When are we leaving?"

"In two weeks."

To reach Seattle in three days, we planned to average 400 miles each day. Driving north on I-5, we made it to Merced, California on our first day of the trip.

We stopped for dinner, got a room with two beds,

and settled in for the night. Ryder showered first and came out of the steam-filled bathroom with a white towel around his waist.

"Don't take long," Ryder said with mischievous grin. "I've got a surprise for you."

I wondered what he meant as I showered, brushed my teeth, and emerged from the bathroom in a towel. We'd chosen our beds when we arrived, his by the door, mine closest to the bathroom. Ryder lay on *my* bed wearing only his towel and the grin.

"Really?" I mumbled.

"Only with you, only you."

We shared our first kiss, and more. Much more.

Continuing our journey to Seattle the next day, we had time to talk.

"I liked last night," Ryder said. "It's definitely different than being with a woman."

"I agree."

"Do you think I could be bisexual?"

"You're the only one who can figure that out."

"You're tender in bed, Pleasant, and I want to explore with you."

One bed sufficed for the two of us at hotels, friends' houses, and family guest rooms for the entirety of the tour. Along the way, Ryder became serious about his possible future, not only with me but with his work.

"I don't know what to do. For much of my life, I've been told I could be a male model. But Pleasant, I'm shy."

"One of your greatest assets is that you're not vain about your looks. You shine in the photos we've taken together. You'll make it as a model if you want to."

"I'd need an agent, right? How do I find one?"

"I know a photographer in Seattle. We'll hire him

for some headshots and sexy photos. You'll have what you need when we get back to San Diego."

"I don't have much money."

"I'll cover it. Pay me back when you're famous."

"It's a deal. You're a star, Pleasant."

"Don't worry. You'll be one soon."

The tour went as planned, and Ryder became a hit with the kids, their teachers, my friends, and my Washington-based family. I fell more in love with Ryder each day. Together late one night in the pagoda of one of my best friend's Japanese garden, I rested my head on his strong shoulder.

Ryder entwined my fingers in mine. "Have you been in love before, Pleasant?"

"Not like this. I've had affairs that led to enduring friendships, but I've always held back. Possibly waiting for you?"

Two frogs croaked from the nearby pond, and Ryder quietly laughed. "That sounds kinda corny."

I chuckled along with him. "I've always wanted to be in love. And now—"

He whispered, "I love you, Pleasant."

We kissed and headed into our guest bedroom. Transcendent sex is like having a *ménage à trois* with the Creator, a trilogy of love. Our lovemaking opened pathways to spiritual realization and bestowed ecstasies more powerful than orgasms. We howled and sighed, laughed and cried. Our bond with each other became sacred. That night we were married in the eyes of God.

Ryder's photos turned out to be spectacular. He signed with a small modeling agency in San Diego and soon began traveling to Japan and several European cities for photo shoots. He kept his apartment in San Diego, and I moved back to Seattle. We agreed on two things—his work came first, and our shared love would continue. Over the next three years, Ryder worked globally for weeks or months at a time. From exotic locales, he sent me letters detailing the settings, fellow male and female models, loneliness, and fun. He ended each handwritten missive the same. *"I love you, Pleasant. Always have. Always will."*

One of his letters contained a photo of a billboard in Greece showing the backside of a gloriously handsome man wearing jeans hugging his beautiful ass. Inscribed on the photo's back: *"These billboards are everywhere in Greece, even on the islands!"*

When he returned home from abroad, Ryder called from San Diego. "Let's fly down to Mexico. I want to spend a week with you on the sand. Just you and me."

We rented a small villa in Puerto Vallarta, meditated together, swam in the sun-warmed sea, feasted on fresh-caught fish, local tequila, and Tecate beer, shared a blanket on the beach during the day, and slept together at night. Sex was relaxed and fulfilling.

Ryder's beauty caught strangers unaware. Many men and women whipped around their heads to stare at him after he'd passed. I often joked, "I should carry chiropractors' business cards in my pocket wherever we went. These people will need neck adjustments."

On the final afternoon of that holiday week, an attractive, middle-aged man held up a book and called to me from his towel a few feet from our blanket. "Are we reading the same novel?"

"*Lonesome Dove* by Larry McMurtry?" I asked, holding up mine.

"That's it. Great book!"

I motioned him over. "Come closer."

He moved his towel next to us. "Hi, I'm Jim."

"Glad to meet you. I'm Pleasant, and this is Ryder."

After a chat about western novels and an appreciation of reading in general, Jim asked, "You two look good together. Are you lovers?"

"We do love each other," Ryder said.

"It shows. How long will you be in Puerto Vallarta?"

"We're leaving in the morning," I answered. "It's been a nice week. What about you?"

"Two more weeks. I'm a talent agent in Los Angeles and represent ten important clients. Only ten. They're all I can handle! One of them is letting me stay at her place for a month. Now, please, tell me about you."

We talked about Ryder's recent travels and shoots and my storytelling. Jim listened intently and shared a bit more about himself. Although he revealed nothing about his clients, it became apparent he was a powerful man in Hollywood.

"Have you guys enjoyed a meal at Le Kliff?"

"No," I said, but I hear it's one of Mexico's finest restaurants. Popular and pricey!"

"Meet me for cocktail at my place. Le Kliff is nearby. I won't be able to join you for dinner, but we can spend a bit more time together. It'll be a perfect beginning to your last night here."

Ryder and I glanced at each other for one second and gave Jim a unison, "Sure!"

Jim wrote a local address on the back of his card. "Show this to the taxi driver. He might not believe you but insist he takes you there. See you at six."

When Ryder handed over the card, the taxi driver looked down at the address and snapped his head back at us. "*¿Vas aqui de Verdad?*"

"Si, señor," Ryder said, "that's *truly* where we want to go."

I climbed into the back seat and announced, "Another adventure, my friend."

Ryder laughed and hopped in beside me. "I like adventures."

The driver wound up narrow roadways into the "Gringo Gulch" neighborhood and let us out at an elegantly carved wooden gate surrounded by a tall adobe wall covered with purple and red bougainvillea blossoms. I pressed the buzzer, and a refined Mexican gentleman wearing black slacks and a white jacket opened the gate. "You must be señor James guests. *Adelante*."

Jim stood by inside the gate and greeted us with a smile. "Welcome to Casa Kimberly. It's Elizabeth's."

"Elizabeth's?"

"Yes, as in Taylor."

My mouth dropped open.

"Richard Burton gave it to her for a birthday present. She doesn't stay here often. See that bridge over the roadway? The Lover's Arch. Richard already owned his villa and had the bridge built to connect the two homes. He died two years ago and willed it to Elizabeth."

"The bridge looks familiar," Ryder said.

"It's a replica of Venice's Bridge of Sighs."

"Wow. I was in Italy last year, and I walked across it," added Ryder. "This is amazing."

"Please come inside. We'll have cocktails in Elizabeth's living room."

Jim, Ryder, and I sat, drank and talked in her tastefully appointed casa. The feminine décor, pastel colors, her personal touches both rich and subtle offered luxury and peacefulness.

As we strolled over the Bridge of Sighs to observe the brilliant night sky, the hills and the sea in the distance, Ryder took my hand. "This is fine, oh, so fine."

Inside Burton's magnificent villa, the swimming pool dominated the courtyard. The three of us lounged on his venerable brown leather sofas while sipping cocktails in this famous man's world of black walnut furniture surrounded by smoky walls—earthy, tasteful, and comfortable.

"You guys should get ready to go," Jim suggested. "I've arranged for a taxi to take you Le Kliff in ten minutes."

"Are you sure you can't join us?" I asked.

"Elizabeth is in Los Angles, and I expect her to call in about an hour. I'm helping organize her AIDS-HIV project. Have a delicious evening and know that I've enjoyed meeting both of you."

After a three-way hug, Ryder and I traveled up the hill for our last meal together.


Perched high on a cliff overlooking the Pacific Ocean, Le Kliff lived up to its stellar reputation. The views were spectacular and the food exquisite. Ryder ordered wild mushroom soup, seared tuna marinated in soy sauce, and a passion fruit crème brûlée for both of us.

Through the candlelight, a darkness dwelled in his eyes I'd never seen before. Halfway through dessert, he began with a story I was unprepared to hear. "I love you, Pleasant, and always will. You've been a gift to me from the day we met. You've challenged me, helped me succeed, and helped me grow. But my life is changing, and, oh God, this is hard…"

My heart melting, I listened.

"You know that I've been with several women in the past few years, mostly models."

"I know. You've told me. You've been figuring things out. Learning what works for you."

"Yes, and I've learned what works for me is the female form. I like sex with you, but I've decided that I prefer women… one woman."

I nodded. That's all I could do.

"Her name's Sylvia. She's Dutch, and she's pregnant. We're getting married next month."

It took several seconds for this latest information to sink in. "Pregnant. Getting married. In San Diego?"

"Amsterdam. I'm moving to Amsterdam, and we'll raise our child there."

"You actually love her?"

"I do, and I want children."

"Okay… I get it… But why didn't you tell me this before? Why the secret until now?"

His eyes wet, Ryder struggled to continue. "This is the hardest part… I've told her about you and what you mean to me… She's frightened."

"Frightened? Frightened of what?"

"You, Pleasant. She's made it clear that she can't, she won't… share me with you. I had to promise that I'd end it with you. It's the only way that Sylvia and I can be happy together and raise our family."

"Without me in the picture?"

Tears streaming down his cheeks, he nodded yes.

That pain-filled night we slept in the same bed, but not together. The next morning during our final prolonged hug in the airport lounge, we spoke no words. He flew to San Diego, and I, home to Seattle.

Once airborne, I began to cry.

A wizened yet perky elderly woman in the seat next to mine asked, "Are you okay, honey?"

"I'll survive."

"A breakup?"

I blew my nose and nodded.

"I'm sorry to hear that. You'll get over it." She patted

me on the shoulder. "We always do."

Ryder remained true to his promise to Sylvia, I never saw or heard from him again. As I write this memory three decades later, my heart expands with love for my friend. He was a gift to me from the universe, a gift of love that will last forever. Our souls remembered when we met. Our souls haven't forgotten.

~ ~ ~

# Riding the Wheel

*You don't have a soul. You are a soul.*
*You have a body.*
~C. S. Lewis~

I HAVE LONG BEEN OBSESSED WITH THE CIRCLE as a practical reality, a unified feeling, and a symbol of the divine. As a bored schoolboy doodling in class, I filled pages with small, medium, and large circles, some alone, others inside each other, some overlapping onto others. I might add a face, a smile, a frown, tiny circles for eyes, and occasionally falling tears. Drawn freehand, my circles weren't perfectly round. I was better at making ovals.

Because of their symmetry, circles represented "natural balance" in ancient cultures. Four thousand years ago, prehistoric people built circles defined with stones, such as Stonehenge in Wiltshire, England, a place of spirit and astronomical observation.

*Enso*, the Japanese word for circle, is a sacred symbol of the Zen School of Buddhism, and a common subject of Japanese calligraphy. Using ink and brush, a friend of mine drew the circle with one stroke and presented it to a professional tattooist who inked the image on his chest over his heart.

"It represents the Circle of Enlightenment," he said when I asked him about it. "It reminds me of the beginning and end of all things. My meditations include what is, and what isn't, inside the enso."

"What's inside?"

"My imperfect life."

"And outside?" I asked.

"An infinite circle. The Creator."

Your soul exists inside and outside your wheel of life. Your soul enters the physical form of your body with your first inhale at birth and leaves with the death rattle of your final exhale. Life is circular. You are born and survive childhood, adolescence, and adulthood. As you mature, you learn the skills required to gain wisdom. You die, death becomes the bridge to life, and the cycle begins anew.

More finite circles and bridges occur during the span of your life. By chance or by destiny, Old Joe built a bridge that mended the circle of friendship with his neighbor. I experienced a full circle of love with Ryder that began, flourished, ended, and propelled me to more circles, bridges, and a deeper appreciation of my life.

Your soul is witness to every breath, word, action, and resulting consequences throughout your entire existence on Earth. Your soul embodies your karmic past, present, and potential futures. You feel your soul in your heart with love that has no limitations. Loving others and receiving their love for you awakens the universal connection with each other and with the Creator.

A meditating friend of mine asked if my Third Eye

Chakra remained open after my experience with Swami Muktananda. As I described in Chapter Four, I told him I'd drove home from the meeting and arboretum experience and collapsed on my sofa. Like the closing of a sliding door, my Third Eye Chakra shut down, and the visions ceased. My nervous system lacked the strength to sustain the phenomenon. Two days later, it reopened for eleven hours. The following week, I cherished a fifteen-hour stretch. Later that month, I saw for a day and a night. Then it was over, or so I thought. Several months later, I realized that my intuitive sight remained partially intact, as it does to this day.

I can see the subtle energy of the chakras at work in a human body, especially when I'm sitting next to a person with whom I have a close connection, or when I look with the *intention* of seeing. Functioning in everyday life would be difficult if I saw a rainbow of energy wheels around everyone walking through an airport!

I understand more about people's lives by watching their breath in action. Or inaction. Breath reveals openings and blockages in the chakras. Breath often tells a person's current life story better than words.

**The Seven Chakras**
Chakra is a Sanskrit word meaning wheel. Originating in Eastern religions and practices, the concept of the chakras encompasses the circle of our physical, psychological and spiritual lives. These seven wheels of energy are located along the spine, from the base—or "perineum," the area between the anus and genitals on the body—to the crown of the head. Besides a unique vibrational frequency and specific function in our human existence, each chakra has a color in the same order you see in a rainbow: red, orange, yellow, green, blue, indigo, and violet.

## 1) The Root Chakra

Located at the base of your spine, your first chakra is associated with the Earth and helps to ground you. It expresses your feelings of survival and safety. The color is red, symbolizing strength and vitality.

## 2) The Sacral Chakra

At the center of your lower stomach, about two inches below your navel, your second chakra also includes the ovaries and testicles. Associated with Water, it's the center of your feelings of well-being and creativity. The color is orange, symbolizing the shifting phases of the moon and its effect on the tides.

## 3) The Solar Plexus Chakra

Located between your navel and the lower part of your chest, your third chakra is the center of your intellect, personal identity, and willpower, as well as the home of your "gut" feelings. Associated with Fire, it connects you to the energy of sunlight. The color is yellow, symbolizing wisdom and power.

## 4) The Heart Chakra

In the center of your chest, your fourth chakra supports the capacity to love yourself and others. Compassion, acceptance, insight, and awareness originate here. Associated with Air, its energy connects the lower and upper chakras, and acts as a bridge between earthly and spiritual concerns. The color is green, symbolizing the earth below and the sky above.

## 5) The Throat Chakra

At the center of your neck at the level of your throat, your fifth chakra is the center of communication, verbal and non-verbal. Associated with Sound, it enables you to express your authenticity, your truth, and your creativity into the world. The color is blue, symbolizing the etheric body.

### 6) The Third Eye Chakra

Located on your forehead between your eyebrows, the sixth chakra is associated with Intuition and Perception. It enhances the subtle energy of insight which allows you to view the world in different ways. The color is indigo, a melding of blue and purple, symbolizing luminescence.

### 7) Crown Chakra

Associated with Higher Consciousness, your seventh chakra is located at the top of your head. Herein lies sacredness and a direct connection with the Creator. It enables transcendence beyond three-dimensional space and time. The color is violet, symbolizing the universe.

### Riding the Wheels of Your Chakras

Balance your breath, and you balance your life. The Native Americans of the Seminole tribe describe the Creator as "Breathmaker"—the Grandfather of All Things. The gift of breath not only creates life but also balances, activates, and connects the energies of your chakras. It's certainly possible the chakras might open spontaneously, but it normally requires practice and patience. The breathing and awareness technique below is a method that works for me and many people that I have counseled. Please take ten minutes and experience it yourself.

*In a quiet space, sit comfortably with your feet on the floor. With your spine straight and in alignment, breathe deeply and fully for a minute. Allow stress to dissipate. Become aware of your body.*

*Focus your attention at the base of your spine and imagine a spinning red wheel of energy. Inhale and send your breath down to your tailbone. Breathe into your Root Chakra for a full minute. Feel the movement, the light, and the strength of your base.*

*Next, move your awareness and your breath to just below your navel. Imagine a spinning wheel of orange light pulsating and sending warmth throughout your Sacral Chakra. Breathe fully, inhaling and exhaling for a minute. Feel the strength of the Root energy combining with your Sacral energy. Remain aware of your body.*

*Now activate your Solar Plexus Chakra. Bring your attention a few inches above your navel and into your chest. Breathe and imagine a spinning yellow energy, glowing and flowing throughout your gut. Breathe for a full minute. Strong emotions are likely to arrive— fear, love, and everything in between. Simply allow the feelings to flow. Don't push them away. Don't deny what is so.*

*Focus your awareness to your Heart Chakra. With the support of the energy from the Root, Sacral and Solar Plexus Chakras, the spinning green energy of the Heart Chakra, infused with light, feels expansive and encompasses the whole of you. Breathe and feel, feel and breathe through these sacred moments. Accept the love flowing in two directions, from you and into you. The universe is aware and bestows unconditional love.*

*Now center your awareness on your Throat Chakra. Imagine a wheel of blue energy clearing your throat, opening your heart, and encouraging you to voice your authenticity. Visualize a universal wind transporting your strong and balanced vibrations far and wide. Stay with this breath and emotion for a minute.*

*Next, shift your focus to your Third Eye Chakra on your forehead between your eyebrows. Imagine the color indigo and breathe into the wheel of light. You'll feel your brain at work, not by thinking about things, but by connecting with universal wisdom. Expand the indigo energy with your breath for a full minute.*

*Finally, let your awareness rise to your Crown Chakra. Herein lies your consciousness, your personal connection to the Creator. Imagine a violet halo of energy rotating directly above your head and feel your enlivened soul. You are deeply, truly, and profoundly loved by all that is. You are a light-being. Breathe your light and love, in and out, for a precious minute.*

*Now rest. Lie down for five minutes and breathe easy. Feel the revitalized energy you've renewed in your being.*

Practice activating and connecting your chakras each day for a month, and you'll help heal the imbalances in your soul life and in your physical life. Your breath, your awareness, and your spine are bridges between the chakras which balance the circle of life. Embodied with the wisdom of the heart, your soul compels you to build bridges with healing words and actions. Breathing through the chakras with awareness creates more love and light in your life.

**Thanks be to Breathmaker, the Creator, and You!**

~ ~ ~

# Story

## CHAPTER NINE

*Those who
tell the stories
rule the world.*

~Hopi Native American Proverb~

# The Miracle

Turkey

L ONG AGO IN THE 15TH CENTURY, the Sultan of the Ottoman Empire ruled over vast areas of the Middle East, North Africa and Eastern Europe, and his dominion continued to expand. He lived in a magnificent palace in Constantinople, an international center of trade and culture that had become known for achievements in science, medicine, and the arts. It was a time of great power, stability, and wealth.

In the midst of all his success, the Sultan was distressed. Each time he picked up the two-year-old child prince and swung him high into the air, the Sultan laughed along with his son, but his laughter contained no joy. The death of his beloved wife two years earlier while giving birth to their son had devastated him, and he had not recovered. As time dragged on, his depression deepened.

The Sultan summoned the royal physician to Topkapi, the royal palace, and confided in him across a wide wooden dining table. The Sultan's face sagged with sadness. His eyes seemed to focus on the space in between the two men. "Every morning I begin each day in sorrow and every evening I end each day in more sorrow."

"Sire, I am profoundly sorry. And every day I worry more about you. You do not eat enough, nor do you sleep soundly. You grow weaker with each passing month. We must find a means to restore your health."

"We? No, *you* must restore my health," the Sultan commanded weakly. "If you cannot help me, consult the greatest minds in our vast lands and find the solution."

"Yes, Your Majesty." The physician bowed and began to back out of the room. "I promise I will do everything in my power to find it."

He called upon a multitude of doctors, scientists, and revered Muslim clerics. None of their suggestions or treatments brought any relief to the Sultan. Neither medicine, science, nor religion could provide the answer, so the royal physician turned to the arts and visited old Akara, the greatest Sufi poet in the Empire.

"Wise Akara, we must find a cure for our Sultan's depression." The physician explained the situation and his failures to solve it. "I'll give you one month to research literature or to question your colleagues and other artists. Perhaps you could even dream of a solution. Go forth and do not disappoint me."

Akara began his explorations the next morning by reading old tomes and ancient books. He traveled to distant cities to question wise men and women. He meticulously noted his dreams in journals during his quest. Three weeks dragged on, and the solution still eluded him. One evening after dinner while sitting around the fire, Akara told his granddaughter of his plight.

She listened intently until he'd finished. "Grandfather, what did you say to me last year when I lost my favorite doll?"

Akara dug into his memories. "I think I told you that your loss would hurt for a while, but you'd get over it."

"Well, you were right. Not only did I get over it, I found a new doll that I liked even better!"

"Of course!" Akara clapped his hands, then rested his palms gently on each of her cheeks. "Granddaughter, you are a *genius!*"

The next morning, Akara rushed to the bazaar, the grand marketplace in the center of the city. Inside the packed corridors, he passed among throngs of people enjoying the fountains, cafes, and places to pray. Most everything imaginable could be purchased in the bazaar—spices, rugs, coffee, clothes, shoes, and all kinds of fruit, vegetables, breads, meats, and desserts. The poet knew his way and wound through the maze of shops to a jewelry artisan who specialized in gold and silver jewelry.

"My friend, I need you to fashion a golden ring," Akara said, "and inscribe it with four words."

"Only four words," asked the jeweler. "And what might they be?"

"This too shall pass."

"Your ring will be ready tomorrow at noon."

When Akara had the ring in his hand, he visited the royal physician at the palace. The physician was skeptical as he viewed the old artist's solution. "This is neither medical nor scientific, but I am willing to try anything. I think you should meet with the Sultan and present it to him yourself. I'll arrange the meeting. Please return tomorrow afternoon."

The next day, the physician met the poet at the gate and escorted him into the throne room at Topkapi palace. Dressed in his black and red robes, his head bound in a bulbous white turban twice the size of his head, the Sultan perched on a wide, hand-crafted, ebony throne inlaid with intricate mother-of-pearl designs.

Akara bowed deeply, kneeled in front of the Sultan,

and shared his story. "Your Majesty, I was speaking with my granddaughter, and she reminded me of the pain of loss. She also reminded me that life is about change. She inspired me to have this golden ring made for you." He bowed again as he offered the ring.

His curiosity piqued, the Sultan inspected the ring, rolled it through his fingers, and read the inscription. "What do these words mean? 'This too shall pass?'"

"From the beginning of time, things change. This ring is meant to make you happy when you are sad, and to make you sad when you are happy. It's the nature of life. Nothing lasts forever."

The Sultan took a deep breath and sighed. "My grandfather used to tell me about a Greek man named Heraclitus, the 'weeping philosopher.' He lived fifteen centuries ago, and is known for his words, 'Change is the only constant in life.'" The Sultan slipped the ring on his finger as a gentle smile crept onto his face. "Akara, I understand. Thank you for this golden gift."

The Sultan wore the ring every day. His depression disappeared, a new precious wife appeared in his life, and he lived to an advanced age. Gazing at the ring, the Sultan often whispered to himself, "My miracle."

~ ~ ~

# The Do-Over

*You raze the old to raise the new.*
~Justina Chen Headley~

## Tucson, Arizona, October 1993

THE BLAZING SUN BORE DOWN on the desertscape causing tall Saguaro cacti to shimmer in the distance. Early Monday morning with the air-conditioner on high, I drove to the eighth elementary school on my ten-school tour and reflected on the revival of traditional storytelling in the twenty years I'd been practicing the art in schools, churches, festivals, and theatres. Other storytellers throughout the nation were on the road as I was, making a living and weaving imaginative spells in a variety of venues. Another day, another school, another paycheck. And always, the feeling of gratitude for bringing fun, suspense, and awareness to children and adults.

"Good on us, each and all," I said aloud.

Sponsored by the University of Arizona, every one of my programs on this tour had gone smoothly. Administrators welcomed me at their schools, teachers showed genuine interest, and hundreds of kids enjoyed the stories.

Had I known what lay ahead, upon arriving at Never-to-be-Named Elementary School, I'd have turned around and headed home. During my thousand-some school visits over the years, I was often greeted with colorful posters proclaiming, "Welcome Storyteller Pleasant DeSpain!" or "We celebrate Book Week with

Pleasant!" No signs appeared as I arrived except the five-sided yellow one that said, "School Crossing."

I parked near the school's main entrance doors to unload my portable sound system, an oriental rug, my wizened wooden stool and a box of my display books.

"You can't stop here!" A middle-aged, female traffic monitor wearing a red-and-yellow vest stomped over to me and pointed to the back of the lot. "Get back in your car and park over there."

"Excuse me?" I was amazed but spoke politely. "I'm the guest artist for today's program, and I need to unload my equipment. It won't take long, and then I'll move my car."

"Move your car right now, or I'll call the police."

"What? Are you serious?"

She blew her whistle in my face.

While thinking of all the things I'd wanted to say, but hadn't, I obeyed the Parking Gestapo and drove to the end of the large parking lot. Three trips later, now wearing a perspiration-soaked shirt, I'd schlepped everything to the front doors and found the office to announce my arrival. The secretary ignored me. She was very busy with what sounded like a personal call. Three minutes later she hung up and glanced over to me as if I was a sweaty vagrant off the street. "What do you want?"

"Good morning. I'm Pleasant DeSpain, here for this morning's program. Grades three to five, I believe."

"There are no programs today. Are you at the right school?"

I handed her the official schedule created by the University of Arizona's English Department. It confirmed I was at the right school on the right day at the right time.

She looked it over and grunted, "Okay, fine." She

gave my paper back to me and started shuffling the papers on her desk.

"May I meet with the principal, please?"

"No. She's busy." Her shuffling got louder.

I felt like a pesky sand fly constantly biting her ankles but pressed on. "Is there a custodian available to help me set up for the show?"

"How would I know?" Irritation coated her words. "You'll probably be in the gym at the end of the hall. He might be there." She waved vaguely in a northeasterly direction as if shooing away a fly.

No custodians in the empty gym, so I hauled all my equipment and boxes down the hallway alone. Most schools provided willing, older boys and girls to help me, and I always found it valuable to interact with kids prior to a show. I quickly discover the school's human—or in this case, inhumane—atmosphere in brief interactions which reveal the general feelings of the people. No luck in the welcome category this morning.

Twenty minutes later, my stool sat on my elegant red Persian carpet centered on the floor in front of the stage. The microphone on the stand was "hot," and the cord long enough for me to walk, gesture, and portray various characters close to my audience. Colorfully displayed on library holders, a dozen of my books graced the wide lip of the stage behind me. I was ready.

A loud buzzer sounded, and the shrill voice of the school secretary echoed over the PA system. "There's a program in the gym this morning. Grades three, four and five, go to the gym."

Normally the youngest and smallest kids in grade three would arrive first to sit on the floor in rows at the front of the stage. Grade four classes would follow, sit behind them, then grade five in the back.

Nothing was "normal" that day.

The fifth graders drifted into the gym, sat up front, and had loud conversations with each other. I scanned the gym for teachers who'd usually direct children into the venue, but of course, none appeared. A mix of third and fourth graders rushed in and squatted with their buddies wherever they liked. I preferred an open aisle down the center of the audience to interact more closely with students while introducing stories. Three hundred kids, the smallest at the back, now filled the complete gym. No aisle. No teachers. Only borderline chaos.

This is a mess, I though. Where are the teachers? The principal? Who will introduce me?'

Most often, the principal or librarian greeted me before the show to welcome me to their "exceptional" school, and we'd discuss the basic content of a brief introduction to help get the program underway.

Not this morning.

Five minutes later, the kids were restless, bored and noisy. Finally, two men and a woman wandered in and stood at the back of the crowd. I assumed they were teachers. One of the men looked at his watch, extended his arm toward me and yelled, "Let's get going!"

Many things are out of the performer's control, and I've dealt with adversity several times during my years of school visits. Sound systems fail, unscheduled fire-drills occur, fights break out, or a child vomits on the kid next to him in the front row after lunch. We who tell, deal with it, and the show goes on. Normally, the storyteller and audience pull together to make the program a success, but I seemed to have driven out of the state of Arizona into the State of Abnormality.

"Quiet, everyone!" yelled the woman standing at the back. "We're already late starting. Listen to the man in front of you!"

That man was me, standing with my microphone in hand, waiting to be introduced. I guessed that was my brief introduction. About half of the audience quieted down and turned their heads toward me, while the other half, the older kids in front, carried on with their conversations. I huddled in my brain and gave myself a quick pep talk. Okay, Pleasant. Take a deep breath. Focus. You can handle this. You always do.

"Hello, everyone! My name is Pleasant DeSpain, and I travel the world searching for good stories to tell. I've brought a few for you today, and I hope you'll enjoy them."

I opened with a short, funny tale, guaranteed to please. It didn't. The teachers at the back engaged in a resounding, show-and-tell discussion about a new mobile phone. The man who'd demanded that I begin, explained in detail the new phone's features to the other two teachers. A large segment of my audience turned around to listen to them.

Based on the feedback and mild applause at the end of my story, I figured that I had maybe twenty percent of my audience's attention and interest.

Better tell 'em a big one, Pleasant. Maybe "Poor Tail-eee-poe," the scary, funny, swamp tale. Snare 'em with your Old Kentucky dialect. And now for those sixty blessed souls who are actually listening...

I started the story and engaged a few more kids. A third of the way into the story, more had jumped on the Pleasant bandwagon. Then three, fifth-grade boys burst into the gym from the back door, ran across the stage, and knocked several of my display books onto the floor. Laughing and leaping off the stage, one of the rascals kicked my largest hardcover book into the front row of the audience. The rascal's friend caught it and threw *Thirty-three Multicultural Tales to Tell* to yet another scoundrel three rows back who then launched the book toward me. It bounced off the floor and landed at my feet on the edge of the carpet.

The teachers at the back, still engrossed in the phone, didn't react to the havoc unfolding in my unruly audience.

Seething with anger, I stopped the story, placed the mike on the stand, bent down to retrieve my book, and farted. Not a small, unobtrusive puff, but a big, boisterous, explosive BRAAAAAP!

Suddenly I had everyone's attention. A spontaneous uproar of laughter rocked the room!

I straightened up, set the book on my stool, and stared at the audience. I didn't speak. It took a full minute of eternity for everyone to settle down. An awkward tension, theirs and mine, hung in the gym.

I retrieved the microphone from the stand and held it close to my mouth. In a self-assured, calm voice, I delivered my decision. "As your guest this morning, I've had enough. You've been unkind. It's obvious that most of you, and certainly your teachers, don't care about the stories I've come to share. It seems that I'm wasting your time. So… I'll do all of you a favor… and leave."

Three hundred children and three teachers remained silent as I gathered my books and walked out. I heard the teachers order the kids back to their classrooms. When the gym was empty once again, I carried my equipment back to my car, alone, and drove away. I felt hollow. Useless. Defeated. It was the first and only time in my career that I'd given up.

When I returned home, I called Mrs. Rodriquez, the woman who'd booked the programs, and explained what had happened. "No need to pay me for this one. It was my decision to walk out."

"I don't believe it, Pleasant! The reviews from your first seven shows are terrific. Every one of the schools loved you. Are you going to complete the tour?"

"Yes, yes. Don't worry. I'll visit the other two scheduled for tomorrow."

Thank God the Creator, all went well the next day.

As I carried my equipment to my car with the help of several students, the school secretary intercepted me in the hallway. "Mr. DeSpain, your tour administrator is on the office phone and wants to speak to you. She says it's important."

I picked up the receiver on the secretary's desk. "Hello? Mrs. Rodriquez?"

"Pleasant, I'm so glad to catch you. The principal of Never-to-be-Named Elementary called to apologize on behalf of her school."

"That's good. It was a disaster."

"She pleaded for me to convince you to return and promised a better experience."

Dumbfounded, I asked, "Why would they ask me back?" Backstage in my mind, another voice asked, "And *why* would you return? Everyone was disrespectful, disinterested, and downright rude. Do you really want to inflict them on yourself *again?*"

"School politics are involved, Pleasant. The whole district has heard what happened and how you were treated. Considering all the positive reviews you've gotten for your work, we told the district superintendent that the University of Arizona could no longer send artists to that school. The principal was dragged across the carpet, and her performance evaluations are on the line. It'll make a difference if you're willing to return."

"I'll think about it and call you tomorrow."

"Well, thank you for at least considering it."

"You're welcome. Goodbye, Mrs. Rodriquez."

A long night ensued. I considered my love of story and how I'd begun my career in order to share that love. I recalled the sixty kids at Never-to-be-Named Elementary who'd been enchanted by "Poor Tail-eee-poe" and the sweet expressions on their faces as they wondered what would happen next as the story unfolded. I had difficulty falling asleep. The next morning, I finally made a decision. Accepting the challenge of an actual "do-over," I returned to the school two days later.

I pulled up to the school's entrance. The custodian and two fifth-grade boys were quickly summoned to help me unload and carry my equipment into the gym. Once we'd set the stage, a message came inviting me to the principal's office.

She looked stressed behind her desk. A woman about fifty, racing toward seventy, a nest of crow's feet beside each eye, glasses perched atop tightly braided, gray hair, and a face that seemed to be singing, "You can take this job and shove it."

"First, Mr. DeSpain, I want to apologize, on behalf of our entire school, for the shameful actions of our students and teachers."

"Apology accepted," I said. "I know schools have good and bad days. Monday must've been a particularly bad one."

"I won't bore you with the details, but it was the worst."

"And unfortunately, you have to spend one seventh of your life on Monday. Some of them are bound to be bad."

"So true, so true," she sighed, paused, then continued. "Second, I promise you that today will be better. Our kids are great kids. Usually they—"

"It's okay. I know how great kids can be. I wouldn't

be here otherwise, nor chosen the life of a storyteller."

"Third, I've talked with our librarian, and we have the funds to purchase a copy of each of your books. We're hoping you'll autograph them for us."

"I'll be happy to. Thank you very much for taking the time to speak with me, but if you'll excuse me, my time is ticking down to showtime."

A few minutes before my presentation, I stood off to the side near the end of the stage to scope out the scene. Needless to say, I was a bit nervous. I'd set up exactly the same as my previous visit. Unlike my previous visit, the students filed into the gym in an orderly fashion— third graders in front, then fourth, and fifth graders in the back. I was pleased with the wide aisle down the center of the seated audience. Nine eagle-eyed teachers stood at the sides and rear of the expansive room. The stares from these tall sentinels added to the already tense atmosphere.

The school librarian strolled up to my microphone, greeted the assembly, and shared her delight in my return. She spoke glowing words about my story collections as she pointed to the parade of books across the lip of the stage. "And Pleasant has agreed to sign each of these wonderful books for our library. You'll be able to check them out tomorrow."

Kids smiled politely, and a few even clapped.

Next the principal again apologized to me on behalf of the school and warned the roomful of children of dire consequences for any misbehavior.

The male teacher with the new phone, making up for Monday's mishap, gave me a generous introduction that concluded with a rousing "Let's give Pleasant a warm welcome!"

Three hundred rigid kids applauded on cue.

Dear God, I thought, what have I gotten myself

into? Surrendering to the situation with a deep breath and inhaling anew, I opened with, "Hello, everyone. I'm sure you'll remember me. I'm the guy who farted."

They laughed long and loud. The teachers laughed. I laughed. The principal managed a stiff smile.

"And I promise not to fart again if you promise to give my stories a chance."

More laughter. Kids scattered through the crowd shouted, "Yes!"

The entire program went without a hitch and ended with "Poor Tail-eee-poe." The gym filled with genuine applause.

Gratitude was given.

Gratitude was accepted.

Such is the power of story.

~ ~ ~

# Your Telling Story

*Fail, fail again, fail better.*
~Samuel Beckett~

## Chiang Mai, Thailand, January 2019

Hello, travelers on the road to light and life… During a trip to the Methow Valley in Washington state, I began this letter months ago in Winthrop, known for the American Old West design of its buildings, wooden boardwalks and cowboy charm. My traveling companion was a long-time brother-by-choice and meditating friend, Paul, who'd been on the path to wisdom for forty-some years.

Sitting on a private deck overlooking the Chewuch River, Paul read a sample chapter of this book and asked me, "Who are you writing your new book for?"

"I've been thinking about the potential readers for the past year. Naturally, I've focused on storytellers, parents, teachers, and meditators as well as those who may want to start meditating. But there are others with whom I'd love to share my experiences."

"And who might those 'others' be?"

"Two come to mind. I often travel in Chiang Mai riding in *songthaews*—a Thai word that literally means 'two benches'—truck taxis with seating in the rear. I'm often joined by back-packers and digital nomads exploring the world and having adventures. Many speak English and conversations ensue as we're sitting close to each other."

I shared this story with Paul about an experience I'd had the previous week.

*One morning, a French couple in their late twenties named Margo and Alex hopped into a songthaew with me. They were heading up to Doi Suthep, a famous temple high on the mountain rising above Chiang Mai. Margo cheerfully started up the conversation.*

*"How long have you been in Thailand?"*

*I shared briefly and asked, "What are you two doing here?"*

*"We love learning about other cultures," Alex said. "And we want to learn to meditate."*

*"That's good! I've enjoyed a meditation practice for forty-six years. It keeps me healthy and happy."*

*"If I'm not being too impolite, how old you are?" asked Margo.*

*"75."*

*"No!" she said, "You look younger."*

*"Thank you. It's one of the gifts of regular meditation.*

*By losing the stress of daily life, I've gained more quality time on earth."*

*"I'd like to hear more of your story," said Alex, "but here's our stop."*

*They climbed off the songthaew and waved goodbye. "Au revoir, Pleasant. Nice meeting you!"*

"I've encountered dozens of Alex and Margo's in the past ten years. This book is for young seekers, as well as those with longer life experience."

"Do you think those two will read it?"

"Once in print, books take on a life of their own. They find their way in the world, just as we do."

Energized by the churning, rumbling river, enhanced by Winthrop's spirit of the Old West, Paul and I had a splendid weekend. As we packed up the car for our trip back to Seattle, Paul put his arm around my shoulder, wished me luck, and predicted the future. "I bet Margo and Alex will find your book."

"I hope so…"


And here you are—young, middle-aged, or old like me—with my book in your hand. You've made it to the final chapter, and we've come a long way together.

I like the sound of the word *together*. Its origin is Late Middle English; its meaning, "to gather." That's what you and I and millions of other folks have done throughout time: gathered true and traditional tales based on an abundance of human experience—yours, mine, and theirs.

Your personal life becomes an integral part of the universal story—shaped and told by you—and is heard by your loved ones, family, friends, enemies, and most significantly, the Creator.

*What has been will be again,*
*What has been done will be done again;*
*There is nothing new under the sun.*

—Ecclesiastes 1: 9

A venerable verse with a valuable message, but I think there *is* something "new under the sun." You are new, living your life, working to create your truth and your authenticity. You may fail and fail again, but so what? If it were easy, the journey wouldn't be worth it.

How many "do-overs" does it take for you to evolve? Within this life or during all your incarnations? You'll probably never know for sure. That's a secret held by the Creator, and yours to discover once you embark on this path.

Maharishi Mahesh Yogi, the founder of Transcendental Meditation, asked his followers, "Are you a cave-dweller or a householder?"

I understood the question. Guided by the desire to discover more about life at an early age, my interest in theology that began in high school, and the realization that I wouldn't marry in this life, I had to choose between the life of a hermit, perhaps as a priest, monk or pastor, and the life of an "ordinary" person dealing with the "real" world. I rejected living and meditating in a cave on the mountain and chose daily life with the confrontations and stress of society. I'm glad to be a "householder" this time around. After accepting the risk and challenges, I'm reaping the rewards. After many disappointments and setbacks, I'm a happy man.

Let me share a Zen tale I heard many years ago.

*A lion was captured in the wild and tossed into a fenced-in camp filled with other lions, young and old. Many of the ferocious beasts had been imprisoned for years. Others born in the camp had been inside their entire lives.*

*Because lions are social animals, they'd created a variety of like-minded groups. One was dedicated to preserving the history and customs of the times before capture when lions were free. Another group banded together to share their religious beliefs and sing beautiful songs about a life after death that promised a fence-free jungle. Some lions preferred the stage and created entertaining shows, while others enjoyed more literary and artistic expressions. A few dangerous groups demanded revolution. They plotted against the guards and every lion who didn't support their cause.*

*The newcomer, astounded by the camp's societal developments, spotted an aged white lioness laying under a tree. Claiming no group identity, she kept to herself.*

*Curious, then newcomer approached the lioness.*

*"Excuse me, but why do you stay apart from the other lions?"*

*"Those simpletons stay busy with everything but what's crucial."*

*"What's crucial?"*

*"Finding the weakness in the fence."*

Now back to you, my sister-brother-friend and fellow seeker. If I were to meet you in person, and we sat comfortably face-to-face with time to spare, I'd say, "Tell me about yourself. Give me the big picture in about five minutes." I wouldn't need your entire story, just the highlights. My philosophy with all story is "Less is more if less is full."

I'd listen fully while hearing your words, observing your body language, and taking notice of your breathing patterns. Words are breath put into form in order to communicate. Words can be deceptive as you craft a story but miss the mark. Breath, on the other hand, tells it like it is, as you are, on that day, and in that hour. Your breath is the foundation of honesty supporting your life journey. Having heard the outline of your current life, I'd ask three questions.

## 1) What's the nature of your fence?

What's holding you back from leaping over the fence, stepping off the wheel, and becoming unified with the Creator? Recall that you are "high born" and are exactly where you should be. You've progressed with your evolution to arrive in this time and place, in a society offering a myriad of pathways for the search for light and life. We both know it isn't easy. What do you think is holding you back? Limited time? Work? Money? Education? Responsibilities? Many responsibilities and so little time?

Most of you are "householders," and have taken on large responsibilities such as jobs, spouses, children, and a mortgage. Your karma is intertwined with the karma of your significant other, his or her family members, your children, your children's children, and so on. Step by step, your karmic story keeps growing.

The same holds true for your past incarnations. With karma building on karma, your dramas, successes, and missteps become more complicated and impossible to comprehend with the three-dimensional mind.

What's possible to understand is that nature demands balance achieved through forgiveness. You don't need details of past events because you're living the entire multi-leveled, ongoing story right now, this time, this life.

And whom do you forgive? It's your story, so first and foremost, *you forgive you.*

## 2) **Whom do you NOT love?**

Tell me the names of one or two people in your current life whom you do not love unconditionally, while keeping in mind that unconditional love is a gift beyond value. As you share your answer, your breath will create a discernible pattern, centered within your Heart Chakra. By noticing the pattern, I gain insight into potentially the largest barrier to your current evolution—the nature of your judgment.

Most of us are judgmental to some degree. No one is "perfect." We instinctively judge others by their appearance, education, job, social status, political beliefs, and religion.

When I participate in storytelling events in America's southern states and am meeting folks for the first time, someone invariably asks, "What's your church?"

"The Church of Human Evolution," I answer, and am usually met with looks of confusion, leading to mistrust.

One man asked me, "Does that mean you're a 'yogatater?"

"Yogatater?"

"You do yoga and meditate? Are you one of those?"

I smiled and nodded. "Yes, sir, I guess I'm one of those."

Without a smile, he replied, "We'll have to keep an eye on you."

*When mistrust comes in, love goes out.*
~Irish Proverb~

What you instinctively mistrust in others is often what you mistrust or doubt in yourself. What angers you about someone else is what angers you about you. The nature of your judgment arises each time you dismiss another because he or she doesn't appear to meet your social, religious, or political standards.

Doubt leads to fear, and where fear exists, love is absent. It takes courage and risk to have open conversations with anyone, especially with the people you love. Sometimes it's easier to share with a stranger who knows nothing about your past. By trusting others, they will trust you and perhaps discover something new and precious in their world... you.

### 3) What's your telling story?

How good is your "poker face"? A **tell** in the game of poker indicates a change in a player's behavior based on their assessment of the cards in their hand. Changes in breathing, voice tonality, facial expressions, and actions with the cards indicate "tells" recognized by experienced players. The most common tell is **weak means strong**. Players who act weak usually have a strong hand to fool their opponents and encourage them to bet higher.

You are telling your story each day while offering a myriad of clues to the observant. Your breath, words, physical gestures, and emotions create an outline of your life—here and now—and your tells reveal that which hasn't yet been healed.

Based on your genetics, current age, and state of your health, how comfortable are you in your physical body? Bodies, like breath, tell it like it is. No amount of makeup, clothing, or disguises can hide the truth.

I've heard thousands of tales told by storytellers and regular folks, in which **strong means weak**. As the story unfolds, the teller puts on a happy face, indicating that all is well when it's not. Most of us carry a burden called "shadow" wherever we go, and as you'll recall from Chapter Three, "The Shadow Knows."

*In the late 1970s, I traveled to Deer Harbor on Orcas Is-
land off the coast of Washington to participate in a week-
long encounter group made up of fifteen men and women
ages 18 to 59. The group objective was to shed fear and
the lack of belief-in-self to gain self-confidence through
self-awareness. After meeting each other during the first
evening meal, we gathered in the lodge's main room and
sat in a circle on the floor.*

*William, our moderator, a middle-aged and mild-
mannered psychiatrist sporting a bushy white mustache
lit the kindling under the logs in the stone fireplace with a
long match. Once the flames began to warm the room, he
explained we would each have five minutes to tell a story
about our lives containing a "hurt" and a "healing."*

*Because Pleasant Journeys, my children's television
show, was still airing, William said, "Let's begin with
Pleasant. He'll show us how to tell a five-minute story."*

*The "hurt" in my story was the fire that had burned
my lower body at eighteen months of age. The "healing"
included being awarded a letter-jacket during my senior
year in high school for cross-country running. I finished
my sharing with thirty seconds to spare. A smattering of
light applause followed.*

*"Good job, Pleasant," William said. "Please take off
your pants."*

*"What?" I asked.*

*"I'd like everyone to see your scars."*

*I removed my pants and walked around the circle of
strangers in my underwear. Whether it was audible or
not, I could feel the gasp of the audience as they witnessed
the damage first hand.*

*Before I could dress, William spoke again. "Tell us
again about being burned."*

*I started in, but within a minute, my legs were shaking*

*and tears streamed down my cheeks.*

*William raised his hand to stop me. "Looks like we have some work to do."*

## When we share our stories, we share our lives.

I'm not your guru or psychiatrist. I'm your partner on the path for however brief or long a time we spend together. The path is wide and presents many options; the journey is long, often involves several incarnations. We may have traveled together before. Perhaps we'll be meeting for the first time.

You and I came into this life with work to do. Don't hold on to the dramas created by disease and accidents or the pain of loss. Remember that *this too shall pass*. If not during this life, perhaps the next. You'll have future opportunities for do-overs.

We've never been alone on the spiritual path. The Creator, our guardians, the humans in our lives, including those with whom we disagree, are walking alongside us, every step of the way. That is the nature of karma.

Karma, and how it works, is one of the major stories of this book. Based on our many pasts, we choose to be born into a family and society that wants us, just as we want them. We're not handed a script outlining the "back stories" of those around us. Not even our own back story. We arrive and immediately forget from whence we came in order to do the work involved in living this life and helping to heal our accumulated karma. The beauty is that it's possible. Not only possible but probable. Each time we take a step forward, the universe rejoices.

*Three things in human life are important.*
*The first is to be kind.*
*The second is to be kind.*
*And the third is to be kind.*

~Henry James~

Every act of kindness and forgiveness creates more light on planet Earth. Every helpful and caring act creates more love, the light-force of the universe.

Heal your heart, and you will heal your past and present karma. Love is more than romance, relationships, marriages, and bonding with your family and children. Love is the foundation of human consciousness. When your heart expands with the warmth of genuine love, you're making progress.

Thank you for sharing this journey with me. Let's continue to seek and find. Continue to heal. Continue to evolve. Together.

With love, light, and life,
Pleasant

# Notes

Stories included in chapters are my retellings of traditional, multicultural, and teaching tales. Motifs given (where appropriate) are from Margaret Read MacDonald's *The Storyteller's Sourcebook: A Subject, Title, and Motif—Index to Folklore Collections for Children* (Detroit: Gale/Neal-Schuman, 1982).

## The Story
Egypt, Chapter One, Page 4

Teaching tales are narratives deliberately created for the sharing of wisdom, and in this story, he who seeks wisdom is in fact, wise. I heard the basic story forty-five years ago and wrote it as I tell it. I've not found other variants in print.

## Pulling the Rope
United States–Connecticut, Chapter Two, Page 14

My neighbor Hank Johnson told me this story in 1967. Being young and inexperienced, I failed to appreciate its strength. Since then I've survived many power struggles by recalling Samuel's solution.

Included in my collection, *Sweet Land of Story, Thirty-Six American Tales to Tell* (Atlanta: August House Inc. 2000) 37–39. An earlier telling.

Other versions are found in *The Housatonic, Puritan River* by Chard Powers Smith (New York: Rinehart, 1946) 258, and in *Westerly (Rhode Island) and Its Witnesses, 1626–1876* by Frederic Denison (Providence, Rhode Island: J.A. & R.A. Reid, 1878) 142–143.

## The Dying Dog
Thailand, Chapter Three, Page 46

A true story shared with me in a Chiang Mai café in 2013 by retired educator, Montague Ball.

## The Boy Who Drew Cats
Japan, Chapter Four, Page 70

Motif D435.2.1.1

Taken with his prosaic stories, I became a fan of the Japanese aficionado Lafcadio Hearn in the 1960s. I've shared this tale hundreds of times to thousands of listeners of all ages.

Included in my collection *The Books of Nine Lives, Tales of Cats* (Atlanta: August House, Inc. 2003) 57–64. An earlier telling.

See *The Boy Who Drew Cats and Other Tales* by Lafcadio Hearn (New York: Macmillan, 1963) 14–20. Another variant is found in *Wonder Tales of Dogs and Cats* by Francis Carpenter (New York: Doubleday, 1955) 195–203.

## The Laughing Brothers
China, Chapter Five, Page 94

A teaching tale, I heard this story in 1981, as told by a follower of the Indian spiritual guru, Sri Rajneesh. Also known as *The Three Laughers*, 17th-century allegorical paintings of the three monks are popular throughout Japan.

See Vedanta: *Seven Steps to Samadhi* by Osho (New Delhi, India: Diamond Books, 2012).

## The Silent Debate
Italy, Chapter Six, Page 128

Motif H607.1 *Discussion between priest and Jew carried on by symbols.*

Variants of this tale are found throughout the world. See *Folktales of Israel* by Dov Noy (Chicago: University of Chicago Press, 1963) 94–97 and *Wisdom Tales* by Heather Forest (Atlanta: August House Publishers, 2003) 42–43.

## Tossing Eyes
The Pemon People of Venezuela, Chapter, Seven, Page 164

Motif A2220. *Animal characteristics as reward.*

The Pemon Tribe lives on the Grand Savannah in the southern Guyana region of Venezuela. The people, who live in circular dwellings made of clay, wood, and palm fronds, enjoy a rich oral tradition. This story not only provides an interesting twist with the arrival of Brother Condor, but also offers the challenge of creating three distinct voices: Crab, Jaguar, and Condor.

Robert Serrano related this tale to me in Tucson, Arizona. Another version is found in *El Tigre y el Cangrejo* by Veronica Uribe (Caracas, Venezuela: Ediciones Ekare-Banco del Libro, 1985). She adapted it from the stories of Father Cesereo de Armellada, who collected traditional Pemon stories for more than thirty years.

Included in my collection *The Emerald Lizard, Fifteen Latin Tales to Tell* (Atlanta: August House, Inc. 1999) 127–131. An earlier telling.

## Old Joe and the Carpenter
United States, Chapter Eight, Page 204

I first heard the bare bones of this, my signature story, from an elementary school librarian in Bellingham, Washington, in 1977. I've simplified the plot and strengthened the ending during my many years of sharing it aloud. In the past 40 years, my version has been reprinted in periodicals and anthologies more than fifty times. I've improved the telling for this work.

Included in my collection, *Sweet Land of Story, Thirty-Six American Tales to Tell* (Atlanta: August House, Inc., 2000) 56–58.

Perhaps the first recorded version is found in *North Carolina Folklore*. Here it is identified as *A Job of Work* by Manly Wade Wellman, Volume III, No. 1, July 1955. In 1951, the story was told to Mr. Wellman by an old bee hunter named Green who lived near Bat Cave in Henderson County, North Carolina.

## The Miracle
Turkey, Chapter Nine, Page 236

Motif D1076.1 *King Solomon's Ring. Makes happy men sad, sad men happy.*

A story told on every continent for thousands of years. See *The Classic Tales: 4,000 Years of Jewish Lore* by Ellen Franjel (Northvale, NJ: Jason Aronson, 1989) 257. *Folktales of Israel* by Dov Noy (Chicago: University of Chicago Press, 1963) 174.

# Pleasant DeSpain

World traveler and "a pioneer of the American storytelling renaissance," Pleasant DeSpain is the author of eighteen multicultural story collections and picture books. He taught speech, literature, and drama for six years in three universities before establishing his career as a professional storyteller in 1972. Pleasant has performed thousands of programs in schools, festivals, and theaters. He wrote, produced and hosted "Pleasant Journeys," a children's television program on KING-TV, Seattle for five years. His unwavering faith in a spiritual awakening has taken him on a life-long search for light and life. Pleasant resides in Chiang Mai, Thailand and upstate New York.

www.pleasant-despain.com